TEACH YOURSELF BOOKS

PHILOSOPHY

Mel Thompson

Acknowledgements

The author and publishers would like to thank the following for their permission to use copyright material in this book:

The Observer, *The Sunday Telegraph* and *The Daily Telegraph* for extracts from their respective newspapers; Chatto and Windus for the extract from Iris Murdoch's *Metaphysics as a Guide to Morals*; Penguin Books Ltd for the extract from *Descartes Discourse on Method*.

Every effort has been made to trace and acknowledge ownership of copyright. The publishers would be glad to make suitable arrangements with any copyright holders whom it had not been possible to contact.

For my daughter, Rebecca

Long-renowned as the authoritative source for self-guided learning – with more than 30 million copies sold worldwide – the *Teach Yourself* series includes over 200 titles in the fields of languages, crafts, hobbies, sports, and other leisure activities.

British Library Cataloguing in Publication Data
A catalogue record for this title is available from the British Library

Library of Congress Catalog Card Number: 94-80154

First published in UK 1995 by Hodder Headline Plc, 338 Euston Road, London NW1 3BH

First published in US 1995 by NTC Publishing Group
An imprint of NTC/Contemporary Publishing Company
4255 West Touhy Avenue, Lincolnwood (Chicago), Illinois 60646-1975 U.S.A.

The 'Teach Yourself' name and logo are registered trade marks of Hodder & Stoughton Ltd.

Copyright © 1995 Mel Thompson

Printed in Great Britain by Cox & Wyman Ltd, Reading, Berkshire.

Impression number   10 9 8 7 6
Year   1999 1998 1997

CONTENTS

The scope of this book

The aims of this book are:

- to map out some of the main areas of philosophy, and to indicate which thinkers have contributed to them;

- to give an outline of some of the arguments that have been put forward;

- to provide an overview of the fundamental concepts and ways in which philosophy has developed over the centuries, so that particular ideas and arguments can be 'placed' in some sort of mental and historical context.

It is unrealistic to expect a book of this length, which tries to introduce a subject as huge as philosophy, to give an adequate account of the thoughts of all those who are mentioned in it. For readers who want to understand more about individual philosophers, there are histories of Western philosophy which offer a systematic outline of both their thought and their historical contexts.

Nor has it been possible to include many extended quotations from original philosophical writings. There are two reasons for this. Firstly, philosophy depends on argument, and arguments take space on the page. A simple quotation giving a thinker's conclusion is less than helpful if the process of thought leading up to it is neglected. In philosophy, a quotation is never long enough. But secondly, it is often difficult to appreciate a text unless one already knows something of the ideas that are expounded in it. As a first step to appreciating philosophical writings, it is as well to get a mental framework within which particular books or passages make sense.

Reading other people's thoughts is no substitute for thinking. If this book attempts to offer 'pegs' upon which to hang a reasoned argument, it is merely a way of assisting the person who is new to philosophy to present his or her case without having to re-invent the philosophical wheel!

INTRODUCTION

———— **What is philosophy?** ————

According to the *Concise Oxford Dictionary*, philosophy is:
> seeking after wisdom or knowledge, esp. that which deals with ultimate reality, or with the most general causes or principles of things and ideas and human perception and knowledge of them, physical phenomena (natural philosophy) and ethics (moral philosophy)

Philosophy is an activity - the attempt to understand the general principles and ideas that lie behind various aspects of life. Political philosophy, for example, asks questions about justice and equality, about how a state should be organised, and about what is meant by ideas such as democracy. It uses many of the same terms that are found in everyday political debate, but it stops to examine them, to probe a little deeper than does the average politician into exactly what is meant, and exactly what the purpose is of the whole enterprise. It asks: What do we mean by this word? How can we know if this is true? What are its implications?

Questions like this are, as the dictionary definition suggests, very general and abstract. This has led some people to think that philosophy is 'dry' and academic. It can be so, but so can most subjects. Take a look at a mathematics text, or a technical diagram - on the face of it they mean little to the outsider, but to someone who understands what is being described, the content can be relevant and exciting.

The same applies to philosophy. It looks at every area of life, and asks the 'big' questions. So you can divide philosophy up into the various subject areas - philosophy of mind, of religion, of science, of politics. You can explore particular styles of doing philosophy, or examine philosophy from an historical point of view, starting (in the West) with the thinkers of ancient Greece (generally Plato and Aristotle) and looking at the way in which it has developed over the centuries.

However it is done, philosophy aims at clarification - of thoughts, concepts and the meaning of language. To philosophise is to think clearly and accurately.

If you study the natural sciences, you are generally able to trace a progression of ideas and a gradual expansion of knowledge. Every now and then there is a 'paradigm shift' and a new way of looking at things is discovered, but such shifts are the exception rather than the rule. By contrast, in reading philosophy you will find that, although you can trace out the progression of ideas, some of the questions explored by the ancient Greeks are still very much debated today, and that some philosophers will be quite willing to dismiss the work of others. Philosophy is always suggesting new ways of looking at questions, new ways of expressing ideas, and new views about the purpose and function of philosophy itself.

Much of philosophy is concerned with language. Indeed, some philosophers see their whole task as linguistic. To appreciate the task of philosophy, however, it is important to distinguish between 'first order' and 'second order' language. Some examples:

First order: 'A caused B.'
Second order: 'What does it mean to say that A caused B?'

First order: 'Is it right to do this?'
Second order: 'What does it mean to say something is 'right'?'

First order: 'God does not exist.'
Second order: 'What is religious language, and how may religious assertions be verified?'

Second order language clarifies first order language. In doing so it also clarifies the thought that lies behind that language. Philosophy is mainly concerned with second order language. It may not be able to tell you if something is right or wrong, but it will clarify the grounds upon which you can make a decision.

——— Why study philosophy? ———

When you communicate with other people, you use language. That language (unless you are simply repeating what you have heard) springs from your ideas and views. These, in turn, will have come from your experience of life and from your education, which may be influenced to a great extent by the accepted attitudes and views of the society into which you have been born.

Philosophy offers you a chance to explore fundamental questions and to see exactly what thinkers in different periods have had to say about them. This in itself is valuable, because it frees you from being limited by the unquestioned assumptions of those around you. To think through issues from first principles is a natural result of having looked at the way in which philosophers have gone about their work. Philosophy also clarifies your thought. The clearer your thinking, the better able you will be to express yourself, and the more accurate your way of examining and making decisions about life.

Secondly, as we saw above, philosophy examines and clarifies language. It is a tool with which to expose nonsense, and express yourself in a way that is as unambiguous as possible. For example, philosophy makes a distinction between 'analytic' and 'synthetic' statements. An analytic statement is known to be true once the definitions of its terms are understood. 2+2=4 is just such a statement. You don't have to go out gathering sets of two items and counting them in order to verify it. You cannot return triumphant and proclaim that you have found a single case which disproves the rule - that you have two sets of two which actually add up to five! Proof, for analytic statements, does not require research or experimental testing. On the other hand, if I say that a certain person is at home, that cannot be true in the same way. To find out, you have to phone or visit. The statement can be proved wrong; it certainly cannot be true for all time.

If someone says 'God exists', is that an analytic or a synthetic statement? Can you define 'God' in such a way that his existence is inevitable? If so, can any evidence be relevant for or against that claim? An argument could go:

> God is everything that exists
> Everything that exists, exists
> Therefore God exists

This argument is sound, but it implies that 'God' and 'everything that exists' are interchangeable terms. This is pantheism (the idea that God and the world are identical) and it is quite logical, but is it what most people mean by the word 'God', and what are its implications for the way we see 'everything that exists'? Of course, things are always changing. There will come a time in the future when nothing that exists now will remain. Does this mean that a pantheistic god will be constantly changing? Can you have a name that stays the same even when the things of which it is comprised are changing? The Greek philosopher Heraclitus, considering the way in which the phenomena of life are always changing, said that a person could not step into the same river twice, since the water of which it was made up was constantly changing. But is a school the same if its buildings are replaced, its staff move on to other posts, and its pupils leave year by year to be replaced by others? Am I the same, even though most of the cells in my body are changing, and my thoughts are constantly on the move? What is the 'I' that remains throughout my life?

In these questions we have touched on some of the central problems of philosophy:

- metaphysics – the study of reality, of what actually exists;
- epistemology – questions about what things we can know, and how we can know them;
- philosophy of religion – the issues that lie behind religious ideas and language;
- philosophy of mind – what is the nature of the self?

This illustrates another feature of philosophy, and a good reason to study it: you can start from any question and find yourself drawn outwards to consider many others. Start from the self, and you find that matters of metaphysics or religion are drawn into your thinking. By using the skills of philosophy, you have the means of integrating your ideas, or relating them, and testing them out against a wide range of topics.

—— Different styles of argument ——

You will find that there are different ways in which philosophy can be presented. Plato, for example, favoured the dialogue form. So his political philosophy in *The Republic* has a range of characters, each of whom presents and argues for a particular viewpoint. Other philosophers examine the meaning of individual words so that, as we take apart a statement, we are able to see all the implications it has.

Some, of course, have tried a more analytic and deductive approach, breaking down accepted ideas into their simplest indubitable elements, and then trying to start from scratch and give an account of what can be known for certain. There is also pure logic, which involves devising artificial languages with which to reveal and set out the logic of our ordinary language.

There was a phase in philosophy – starting early in the twentieth century – where the sole task of philosophy was said to be the meaning of words. All philosophy was said to be about language, and once the linguistics was sorted out, all else would follow. Today that view is giving way to a broader perspective. Philosophy is indeed about language, and it is essential to understand the language you use, but it is also important to rise above the language and individual words, to explore the basic ideas and concepts to which it gives rise, and from there to explore features about the world that would not have come to light without that process of serious thinking.

Of course, philosophers do not always agree about how to do philosophy, or what is of value. The late A J Ayer, interviewed about his work in 1980, commented in his usual direct way on the work of various philosophers, saying of the philosopher Heidegger's language about 'the Nothing' that it seemed to him to be 'sheer rubbish' and that people might sometimes be impressed because they like to be mystified. [Interview with Miriam Gross; the *Observer* 24 February 1980 p.35.] In chapter 7 we shall be looking briefly at the work of Heidegger. You may feel inclined, after reading that, to agree with Ayer, or you might feel that Heidegger is describing something of greater importance than Ayer's rational analysis of what can be known and described. The essential thing to realise at this stage is that not all philosophers agree either on the topics about which to philosophise, or the way to set about it, or the conclusions reached.

Philosophy is not monolithic. There is no body of established and unquestioned work. Rather, it is an activity; and an activity which often raises more questions than it solves.

——— Areas of philosophy to be ———
included in this book

There are two fundamental questions with which philosophy is concerned:

1. What is the nature of reality? What is the structure of the world in which we live? These questions are to do with metaphysics: general and profound questions that lie beneath the sort of evidence that science examines.

2. What can we know for certain? What constitutes sound evidence? Are there any absolute truths? This is termed epistemology: the theory of knowledge.

And alongside both of these there is the ongoing question about language. Philosophy has to use language, but it also analyses it, challenges it, probes its limitations and the way in which statements can be proved or falsified.

In chapters 1 to 4 we shall be looking at a range of philosophical issues. The theory of knowledge appears to have a chapter to itself – but metaphysics and language are found in all of them, and the theory of knowledge is also relevant to the other topics. Issues of religion, the mind and science are central to any serious study of philosophy, and they illustrate the way in which the basic philosophical questions about language and meaning are applied to particular issues.

But human beings not only seek to understand their world, they also live in it, make choices in it, and organise themselves into societies. Philosophy therefore addresses two other practical areas of life – ethics and politics. These will be examined in chapters 5 and 6.

In chapter 7, there is a brief look at a range of other philosophical approaches, to give a 'taste' of what is available in the world of philosophy today. The phenomenology of Husserl, for example, and existentialism are important for understanding Continental philosophy. Formal logic is an area of which students need to be aware, at least glimpsing the way in which the logic of arguments may be set out and debated. Aesthetics examines art and tries to define what we mean by beauty. Finally, there is a brief look at other areas of modern Continental philosophy, such as deconstruction or postmodernism, which have implications for literature and art as well as philosophy.

— **Philosophy and Western thought** —

Each generation builds on the ideas and values of the preceding one; sometimes by way of rejection and change, sometimes by conformity and development. But in any case it is not possible, for example, to live in Western Europe, or the United States, without having your language and ideas influenced by generations of thinkers. To be aware of your heritage, sensitive to the way in which ideas and the institutions based on them have grown and developed, gives you a greater appreciation of your own culture – whether that appreciation leads you to criticism or acceptance of all or any of its ideas.

It is possible to approach philosophy from a number of different directions. One way is to list the main issues with which it is concerned and then to look at the way in which different philosophers have examined them. Another is to take an historical overview. In many ways this latter is the most rewarding, for it reveals the interests of each period in history. It shows the way in which the presuppositions of thinkers arise out of their social context.

But it reveals something else. Although there is progress in philosophy, as each generation learns from the last, there is also a sense in which philosophy is required to return time and again to the same central dilemmas.

In the introduction to his overview of Western philosophy, John Shand says:

> It is characteristic of philosophy that it goes back to where most other subjects begin and then probes still further back in its inquiries. Philosophy discusses enduring problems arising from life and thought. It is one of the attractions of philosophy that it connects thinkers of otherwise different historical ages and finds in them the same fundamental problems.
>
> [*Philosophy and Philosophers* J Shand Penguin 1994 p.ix.]

In one sense, this could lead to frustration. Why study Plato? Why should syllabuses devides by examining bodies be dominated by the long dead – Plato, Aristotle, Descartes, Hume – with texts from Russell, Ryle and Ayer tipping older issues into the twentieth century?

It is important to recognise that the historical perspective, as Shand goes on to demonstrate in his book, reveals the many layers of thought that are still relevant to each of the problems with which philosophy is concerned. Plato's views of society or his way of understanding the nature of reality; Aristotle's idea of causality; Descartes' quest for certainty - all remain relevant, because all reflect an approach which can still be taken seriously, even if the terms in which it would be expressed today are different from those of the original thinkers. As Shand indicates in the quotation given above, philosophy probes into the presuppositions of any argument or claim. It looks at it in context, and then it delves into the ground from which it comes, the arguments used to justify it, and its implications. Issues of truth are not historically limited. Something may have appeared valid at one time, and be justified by sound reasoning, and yet it may not be true in any absolute or permanent sense.

The philosopher Karl Popper, in examining the way in which science makes progress, laid stress on the fact that a theory, if it is truly scientific, must be capable of being falsified. Progress is made, not by continually heaping up examples of where a theory works, but of finding examples of where it fails. The failure of one theory gives birth to the next - and the same has been true of philosophy. Each generation of philosophers has examined established ideas, and, by showing their limitations, is able to formulate new ones.

For those who crave definitive answers, philosophy is likely to prove a source of constant frustration. For those who constantly ask questions, and are prepared to examine and modify their views, it is a source of fascination and a means of sharpening the critical faculties.

For many years, much of the philosophy taught in Britain and America was dominated by a very limited view of its function. Philosophy claimed almost no content of its own; its task was to analyse and clarify statements made in other disciplines and by people in general. It took no leaps of intuition, opened no new vistas on the world, but sought a very detailed, supportive role. An historical perspective, and the range of topics tackled over the centuries, show that philosophy is much broader in its scope and wider in its appeal. And the traditional range of topics considered – epistemology (theory of knowledge), philosophy of religion, philosophy of mind, philosophy of science, ethics - is valuable for showing this broader scope of the philosophical enterprise.

This book – like froth on the tip of a wave – is carried forward by the whole movement of thought that stretches back at least two and a half thousand years. What it seeks to do (while acknowledging its limitations of coverage and depth) is to point to the reality of the wave, and the general direction of the water within it. A society without philosophy would be cut off from its own roots; it would have to start from scratch time and time again to sort out its values and its self-understanding. With philosophy, that process of sorting out is shown in its historical and logical perspectives. With philosophy, you start at an advantage, you look at each problem with the benefit of knowing something of the accumulated wisdom of some of the best thinkers in Western culture.

—————— Worth the hemlock? ——————

One of the most remarkable moments in the history of Western philosophy is the death of Socrates in 399BCE. The event is recorded by Plato, whose respect for his teacher was such that he set out most of his philosophy in the form of dialogues in which Socrates plays the central role. Charged with impiety and condemned on grounds of corruption of the young, Plato (in *Crito*) presents Socrates as willing to accept death (by drinking a cup of hemlock) rather than try to escape. For Plato, reason and the freedom of the individual to live in accordance with it took priority over the social and political order. Indeed, as he was later to expound in *The Republic*, justice and the institutions of state should be based on reason, and rulers should be philosophers, willing and able to apply reason with disinterested objectivity.

The task of the philosopher was not peripheral to life, but central. To cease the questioning and challenging of accepted concepts was unthinkable; Socrates had chosen to accept death rather than escape from Athens. He is presented as calm, rational and a man of absolute integrity.

Philosophy can be a frustrating discipline. Sometimes it appears dry and remote from life. Sometimes it takes the role of linguistic handmaid, clarifying the terms used by other disciplines without appearing to offer anything of substance to the sum of human knowledge. Sometimes philosophers insist in setting down their thoughts in a style that obscures rather than clarifies. From time to time, one may be tempted to ask 'Is it worth it? Why not settle for established thoughts and values, however superficial? Why make life difficult by constant analysis?' or, in the case of Socrates, 'Is it worth the hemlock?'

That I leave the reader to judge.

1

WHAT CAN WE KNOW?

There are some basic questions that have occurred throughout the history of philosophy and which affect the way in which many different topics are considered:

- What can we know?

  This question is about the basic features of existence; not the sort of information that science gives about particular things, but the questions that lie beneath all such enquiry: questions about the fundamental nature of space, time or causality; about whether concepts like 'justice' or 'love' have any external, objective reality; about the structure of the world as we experience it. In the collected works of Aristotle, such questions were dealt with after his material on physics and were therefore called 'metaphysics'.

But as soon as we start considering metaphysics, another question arises:

- How can we know it?

  Is there anything of which we can be absolutely certain? Do we depend entirely on our senses, or can we discover basic truths simply by thinking? How can we justify or prove the truth of what we claim? All such questions are termed 'epistemology' – the theory of knowledge.

But when we deal with metaphysics or epistemology, we have to communicate our thoughts in some way. The medium for this is language. We ask 'What can we say?' and 'How can we say it?' The study of the nature of language, and the way in which statements can be shown to be true or false, is another constant preoccupation of philosophy.

In this chapter we shall be examining something of these three things – metaphysics, epistemology and language. If you have a sound knowledge of these, then it becomes much easier to examine the way they are applied to the various topics to be considered later – God, the mind, politics. You will find that the same fundamental problems occur in all areas of study.

But first, an outline of some basic problems:

For metaphysics:

A very basic problem here concerns 'reductionism', and the existence of, or reality of, complex entities or general concepts.

Consider these questions:

- How does a painting relate to the individual pigments or threads of canvas of which is it made?
- How does music relate to vibrations in the air?
- How does a person relate to individual cells in his or her body?
- How does a nation relate to the citizens of which it is made up?

A 'reductionist' approach to metaphysics takes the 'nothing but' view, e.g. that music is 'nothing but' vibrations in the air.

If you believe that the ultimate reality is matter – the solid external world that we experience through our senses – then you are probably going to call yourself a 'materialist'. On the other hand, if you hold that the basic reality is mental – that the world of your experience is really the sum of all the sensations and perceptions that have registered in your mind – you may be called an 'idealist'.

These questions can be relevant to practical decisions. When, on Christmas Day, the British and German soldiers facing one another in the First World War came out of their trenches, played football together and shared cigarettes, they ceased to be merely representatives of nations and acted as individuals. Later, they returned to their trenches and continued to kill one another.

'Which is more real? Which should guide action? – to act as individuals, and to frame political decisions on the basis of what individuals want, or to give primacy to the 'nation' or the 'class', even if individuals have to suffer as a result?' That is a matter for ethics, but we can go further and ask 'Do nations actually exist? Is there any such thing as society, or are there just people and families?' These are fundamental questions, but they have important practical consequences.

For epistemology:

A basic issue here is whether the basis of everything we know is given in the data that comes to us through our senses, or whether all such data is fallible, and the only certainties come through that which is known by the mind.

Empiricism – all knowledge starts with the senses

Rationalism – all knowledge starts with the mind

For language:

A key question for language is 'verification'. How do you show that a statement is true?

- Do you set out bits of evidence that correspond to each of the words used? (An empiricist might encourage you to do that. A reductionist might say that your statement was nonsense unless you could do it!)

- Do you point to the internal logic of what you have said?

The distinction between synthetic and analytic statement has already been mentioned. When we come to examine ethical language, for example, we will see that language can be used in many different ways, and that verification is by no means straightforward. An average line of poetry, a joke, a command or the whispered endearments of lovers can quickly dispel any simple theory of verification.

Questions of epistemology, metaphysics and language cannot always be neatly separated from one another, and in this chapter we shall move from one to another. What you know and how you know it are always going to be closely linked.

——————— Are you certain? ———————

Whenever I experience something, that experience involves two things:

1. The sensations of sight, sound, taste, touch or smell, all of which seem to me to be coming from outside myself, and to be giving me information about the world.

2. My own senses. If I am partially deaf, I may be mistaken in what I hear. If I am colour-blind, I will not be able to distinguish certain patterns, or appreciate the subtleties of a multicoloured fabric. If I am asleep, all sorts of things may go on around me of which I am quite unaware!

Imagine that I am taken to a police station and questioned about something that is alleged to have happened in the recent past. I give my account of what I have heard or seen. If it sounds credible, or agrees with the evidence of others, I am likely to be believed. On the other hand, the police may ask 'Are you sure about that? Is it possible that you were mistaken?' The implication is that, even if I am trying to be accurate and honest, the senses may be mistaken, and there may be two quite different ways of interpreting an experience.

When philosophers ask, 'What can be known for certain?' or 'Are the senses a reliable source of knowledge?' they are trying to sort out this element of uncertainty, so as to achieve statements that are known to be true.

Basically, as we saw above, there are two ways of approaching this problem, corresponding to the two elements in every experience.
- **Empiricists** are those who start with the sensations of an experience, and say that all of our knowledge of the world is based on sensation.
- **Rationalists** are those who claim that the basis of knowledge is the set of ideas we have – the mental element that sorts out and interprets experience. The mind is primary, and the actual data of experience are secondary.

But before we look at these approaches in more detail, let us be clear about a category of things that we can know for certain. If I say that 2 + 2 = 4, there is no doubt about the truth of that statement. Mathematics and logic work from agreed definitions. Once those are accepted, certain results follow. They do not depend upon particular situations or experiences.

In general terms I can say that: If A = B + C, and if B and C are contained in, or implied by, the definition of A, then that statement will always be true. Understand the words and you understand its truth. Statements that are true by definition, although they are important, need not therefore detain us.

Descartes (1596-1650)

Descartes used the method of systematic doubt, by which he would only accept what he could see clearly and distinctly to be true. He knew that his senses could be deceived, therefore he would not trust them, nor could he always trust his own logic. The one thing Descartes could not doubt was his own existence. If he doubted, he was there to doubt; therefore he must exist. The famous phrase which expresses this is *cogito ergo sum* ('I think, therefore I am').

This quest for certainty is set out in *Discourse on Method* (section 4).

I had noticed long ago... than in matters of morality and custom, it is often necessary to follow opinions one knows to be highly doubtful, just as if there were no doubts attaching to them at all. Now, however, that I intended to make the search for truth my only business, I thought it necessary to do exactly the opposite, and to regard as absolutely false anything which gave rise in my mind to the slightest doubt, with the object of finding out, once this had been done, whether anything remained which I could take as indubitable. And so, because our senses sometimes deceive us, I made up my mind to suppose that they always did. Then, since there are men who fall into logical errors when they reason, even in the simplest geometrical matters, I reflected that I was as fallible as anyone, and rejected as false all the arguments I had hitherto regarded as conclusive. Finally, in view of the fact that those very same ideas, which come to us when we are awake, can also come when we are asleep without one of them then being true, I resolved to pretend that everything that had ever entered my mind was as false as the figments of my dreams. But then, immediately, as I strove to think of everything as false, I realised that, in the very act of thinking everything false, I was aware of myself as something real; and observing that the truth: *I think, therefore I am*, was so firm and so assured that the most extravagant arguments of the sceptics were incapable of shaking

it, I concluded that I might have no scruple in taking it as the first
principle of philosophy for which I was looking.

[edn. Penguin Classics, p.60f]

Descartes could doubt even his own body, but, while doubting, he
could not deny himself as a thinking being. All else was open to the
challenge that he could be mistaken.

In many ways, this argument of Descartes represents the starting
point of modern philosophy (modern, that is, as compared to that of the
ancient Greeks and of the medieval world), not because later thinkers
have been in agreement with him, but because, challenged by his
scepticism, they have followed his quest to find the basis of certainty
and knowledge. In other words, Descartes sets the agenda for
epistemology.

But do we need to be that sceptical about what we experience?

Russell (1872-1970)

A clear explanation of the way in which experience can be analysed
and questioned is set out in Russell's book *The Problems of Philosophy*.
He examines the table at which he sits to write. He observes that its
appearance changes in different light and from different positions, and
comes to the conclusion that our sense perceptions (the actual
experiences of colour, shape and texture) are not the same thing as the
table itself (otherwise we would have to say that the table becomes
black once the light is turned out, or gets smaller when we walk away
from it), but that we have to infer the table from our perceptions. He
therefore distinguishes sense data from the 'physical object' which
gives rise to them.

He refers to Bishop Berkeley (1685-1753), who argued that there is
nothing given in our perception of something which we can show to
continue even when nobody is perceiving it. In order to maintain
continuity when things are not being observed, Berkeley used the idea
that they were being observed by God. In other words, what we call
matter (external objects) are only known to exist in dependence upon
minds that perceive them.

Having commented on Descartes' systematic doubt, Russell points
out that common sense suggests that there are ongoing objects, and
that they do continue to exist when not being observed. He has the

example of a cloth thrown over a table. Once that is done, the table cannot be observed, but it is implied by the shape of the cloth, apparently suspended in mid air. He also considers the situation where a number of people look at the same table. Unless there were some underlying reality, there seems little reason why everyone should see the same thing.

He takes the idea of a cat which becomes equally hungry whether it is being observed or not. If it did not exist except when being observed, this would not make sense. Indeed, he points out that the cat's hunger is something that I cannot observe directly, and therefore (in terms of sense data) it does not exist.

All this leads him to accept the idea, given in an instinctive belief which he has no reason to reject, that there is indeed an external world which gives rise to our sense experience.

──── **Things?** ────

The essential thing to grasp in this whole section is that sense data are not simply 'things'. They depend upon our senses and relationship, as well as on that which is being described.

The rationalism/empiricism debate can be seen by contrasting Descartes' views (as briefly outlined above) with those of John Locke, Bishop Berkeley and David Hume.

Locke (1632-1704)

Locke (see *Essay Concerning Human Understanding*) starts from the same position as Descartes – the desire to know what the mind can comprehend and what it cannot. But his conclusions are radically different. He claims that there are no such things as innate ideas, and that all that we know comes to us from experience, and from reflection upon experience.

Locke holds that there are primary qualities (solidity, extension, motion, number) and that these qualities inhere in bodies. There are also secondary qualities (colour, sound, taste, etc) and these depend upon the perceiving person.

He holds that we can know of the existence of bodies through our senses. The sense data we receive cannot be subjective, because we do not control them. (This is similar to the position outlined by Russell as he looks at his table – because others see it as well as he, he concludes that the table itself cannot depend upon his own sensation, even if the actual data he receives does so.)

Locke was certainly influenced by Descartes. He had to accept that there was an unknown substance, for he could know nothing directly, only through his senses. In this he anticipated to some extent the more general conclusions of Kant, who later made the radical distinction between things as they are in themselves (noumena) and things as we perceive them (phenomena). The radical difference between Locke and Kant is that Kant thinks that space, time and causality are contributed by the perceiving mind. Locke thinks that space and time are in the external world.

Berkeley (1685-1753)

Bishop Berkeley argued for 'idealism', which is the theory that everything that exists is mental. This sounds an unlikely view to hold about the world, but it follows from the way in which we perceive things. An idealist might argue as follows:

- All we actually know of the world are sensations (colour, sound, taste, touch, the relative positions of things that we perceive). We cannot know the world by any other means. For us, these sensations are what we mean by 'the world'.

- All these sensations are 'ideas': they are mental phenomena. (The colour red does not exist independent of the mind perceiving something of that colour.)

- Things are therefore collections of these ideas; they exist by being perceived.

The obvious problem for Berkeley was showing how something can exist while not being perceived:

A silly example:

I am aware of a tree in front of me. I see the trunk, branches and leaves with their different colours. I may reach forward and touch the bark. The tree, for me, is the collection of all these sensations. In order to test out idealism, I shut my eyes, put my hands by my side, and attempt to cut off all sensations of the tree. Convinced that the tree no longer exists, I step forward. The tree immediately re-appears in the form of an acute pain in the nose and forehead!

But, what does it mean to say that the tree exists in the moment between shutting my eyes and hitting the trunk?

It is possible to say that an object continues to exist if it is being perceived by someone else; but what if nobody perceives it? Berkeley's answer to this is that the tree continues to exist only because it is being perceived by God.

In thinking about Berkeley's theory, it is worth reflecting on where sensations are located. Because they take place as a result of brain and sensory activity, Berkeley says that they are mental – in effect, that they are taking place 'in' the mind. But just because a sensation varies with different conditions, as colours change with different lighting, does that imply that the whole of what we mean by colour is subjective?

Berkeley also held that there are no abstract general ideas. If you think of a triangle, you are thinking of a particular triangle. It shares its qualities with other triangles, but there is no concept of triangle that does not spring from some particular triangle. What we think of as a 'universal' is just a set of qualities abstracted from particulars.

NOTE:

Few things are new in philosophy. This discussion (as we shall see shortly) can be traced back to Greek thought and illustrated by the differences between Plato and Aristotle on this matter. If you believe that universals are 'real' then you are likely to be called a 'realist', but if you think that universals are only the 'names' we give to groups of individuals, you are a 'nominalist'.

Hume (1711-1776)

Hume takes a radical empiricist position, in which all knowledge is derived from sense experience. Hume made the important distinction (which we have already discussed) between what we have called analytic and synthetic statements. In other words, between:

- those statements that show the relationship between ideas. [These are known to be true *a priori* (before experience) because their denial involved contradiction, e.g. the propositions of maths and logic. They offer certainty, but not information about the world.]

and

- those which describe matters of fact. [These can only be known *a posteriori* (after experience). They are not certain, but depend on empirical evidence.]

This leads to what is known as Hume's Fork. In this, you may ask of a statement:

- Does it contain matters of fact? If so, relate them to experience.
- Does it give the relationships between ideas?

If neither, then it is meaningless.

Hume's argument concerning evidence runs like this:

- I see something happen several times.
- I therefore expect it to happen again.
- I get into the mental habit of expecting it to happen.
- I may be tempted to project this mental habit out onto the external world in the form of a 'Law' of physics.

So, for example:

'A causes B' could be taken to mean 'B has always been seen to follow A'. It might be tempting to say 'Therefore B will always follow A', but this would imply that nature is uniform, and you can never have enough evidence for such an absolute statement.

To the statement 'Every event must have a cause', Hume would say:

- it can't be justified by logic, since its denial does not involve self-contradiction;
- it can't be proved from experience, because we cannot witness every event.

What, then, are we to do? Hume says that we can accept the idea of causality because it is a habit of the imagination, based on past observation. This may seem obvious, but an important distinction has been made between claiming that something *must* be the case, and saying that, in practice, we have always found it to be the case.

In section ten of *An Enquiry Concerning Human Understanding* (where Hume is considering miracles) he sets out his position about evidence:

> A wise man ... proportions his belief to the evidence. In such conclusions as are founded on an infallible experience, he expects the event with the last degree of assurance, and regards his past experience as a full proof of the future existence of that event. In other cases, he proceeds with more caution: He weighs the opposite experiments: He considers which side is supported by the greater number of experiments: to that side he inclines, with doubt and hesitation; and when at last he fixes his judgement, the evidence exceeds not what we properly call probability.

Hume's approach is also valuable in assessing the question of whether or not the external world exists, and whether we could prove it to exist. He says that it cannot be proved, but gives two features of experience which lead to the idea being accepted – constancy and coherence. I see that objects remain in the same place over a period of time, and I assume that they remain there even when not observed. Also, I may see someone at different times in different positions, and I infer from this that they are moving about. In other words, the assumption that the world is predictable enables me to fill in the gaps of my own experience. Once again, however, the key thing to remember is that this is not something that can be proved.

Kant (1724-1804)

An important figure in this debate is Kant. He held that certain features of experience, including space, time and causality, were imposed by the mind on experience. Take the example of time. When I see a sequence of things, I say that time is passing and that thing one follows another. But where is that time? Is it something that exists 'out there' to be seen? Kant would argue that time is one of the ways in which my mind organises experience. We make sense of the world by organising it into these categories.

- 'But what happened before the 'Big Bang'?' is an example of the mind trying to impose the category of time on something to which scientists try to tell us it cannot be applied. However much I accept the idea of space and time coming from that 'singularity', my mind rebels and demands yet more space and time before and beyond it.

I am given a description of the universe, and ask 'But what lies outside it?' If I am told that nothing lies outside it, I become confused, for my mind automatically tries to imagine an expanse of nothingness stretching outward from what is known.

The same is true for causality. We assume that everything has a cause. Even when we have no evidence of a cause, we know that one will be found eventually – because that is the way the world works. Kant would say that it is the way the mind works. We impose the idea of causality on our experience. Kant made the important distinction between what we perceive with our senses (which he called phenomena) and things as they are in themselves (which he called noumena).

• One way of appreciating this distinction is to consider yourself. The real 'you' is a noumenal reality, you exist in yourself, irrespective of other people's perceptions of you. But you are a phenomenal reality for everyone else – all they know about you is what you show to them. Now ask yourself 'Am I really nothing but the sum total of what others can see of me? Is there something of me which I know, but which I cannot ever fully show to others?'

In many ways, Kant's philosophy can be seen as an attempt to take seriously the claims of the Empiricists (e.g. Hume) that everything depends upon experience, and is open to doubt, but to do so in the context of Newtonian physics and the rise of science. Science seeks to formulate laws which predict with certainty, and causality is an essential feature of Newtonian science. How then can you take an empiricist view of our knowledge and also accept the findings of science?

Kant sought to achieve this through what he called his Copernican Revolution. Just as Copernicus totally changed our perception of the world by showing that the Earth revolved round the Sun and not vice versa, so Kant argued that certainties of space, time and causality (on which Newtonian physics was based) was not a feature of the unknowable world of things as they are in themselves (noumena) but of the structures of our own perception (which gave rise to phenomena). In other words, the world of our experience is shaped by our own means of perceiving and understanding it. This was his way of reconciling these two important elements in the consciousness of the eighteenth century, and it has many implications for later thought.

IN OTHER WORDS:

- What we know of the world depends on our senses and we interpret them.
- There are no simple 'facts', totally independent of our perception: not just qualities like colour and texture, but space, time and causality too – all depend upon the way in which human beings perceive things.
- Therefore it is difficult to say what we can know for certain.

Appearance and reality

As we have already seen, metaphysics examines what lies behind, or is implied by, our experience of the world. It explores general ideas such as 'goodness', 'honesty' and 'beauty' and tries to say what role to play in our understanding of reality. Without metaphysics, the world is just a jumble of experiences without overall coherence.

Of course, it is possible to claim that our experience of the world is a jumble of sensations without overall value, sense or direction. That is a rejection of all metaphysics. It is equally possible to seek for, and have an intuition that there should be, some overall sense of reality and unity in the world; a sense of the absolute reality, the understanding of which will give guidance for the interpretation and valuation of all individual experiences. This sense of overall coherence may be expressed in terms of God, or it may not. But in either case, what is being done is metaphysics.

The debate about knowledge and reality predates Descartes, even if he is a convenient starting point because of his radical doubt. The ancient Greeks were concerned to explore both the nature of experience and the words we use to describe it.

Pre-Socratic philosophers

The philosophers Plato (427-347BCE) and Aristotle (384-322BCE) are the most important of the Greek thinkers for the subsequent history of Western philosophy, and they set much of the agenda for those that followed. Plato took his inspiration from Socrates (470-399BCE), whose ideas we know only through his appearance in Plato's dialogues.

But before Socrates there were a number of philosophers who were concerned with metaphysics from what would later become a 'scientific' standpoint. They sought the principles that lay behind all natural phenomena.

Although there is no scope here to discuss them individually, they are covered in most histories of Western philosophy, and are well worth studying. Of particular interest are the views of the 'atomists', who (anticipating Newtonian physics) thought of all material objects as made up of atoms, and who recognised that many secondary qualities (colour, etc) were dependent upon the perceiver, rather than qualities inherent in what was perceived.

There was also a fascination with the ideas of permanence and change. Heraclitus is attributed with the idea that one cannot step into the same river twice, for the 'river', being a collection of particles of water, is constantly changing. Does the river have any reality other than the drops of water of which it is formed? Is it a permanent reality, even if the actual water changes?

The earliest thinkers (Thales and Anaximander are from the sixth century BCE) may seem to have only primitive ideas of cosmology and physics. But what is remarkable is that they should have tried to give an overall explanation of the world: to make it a 'cosmos', an unified, rationally understood world. There had been, and continued to be, myths and images by which the world could be explored and given meaning, but these early philosophers set out to formulate rational principles about the world's fundamental structure and composition.

Plato (427-347BCE)

In *The Republic* Plato uses an analogy to illustrate his view of human experience. People sit near the back of a cave, chained so that they cannot turn to face its mouth. Behind them is a fire, in front of which are paraded various objects. The fire casts shadows of these objects onto the cave wall, and this is all that they can see. This corresponds to the normal way in which things are experienced: shadows, not reality itself. But then a prisoner is freed and can turn round, seeing first the fire and the objects which cast the shadows, but then, being dragged up to the mouth of the cave and into the sunlight the prisoner gradually adjusts to see the sun itself. Only then is it clear that the former way of perceiving was only of shadows. This, for Plato, corresponds to the journey from seeing particular things, to seeing eternal realities of which the particulars are copies.

In Plato's dialogues, Socrates debates the meaning of words. What is 'justice'? Plato takes the meaning of a word to correspond to some permanent external reality. 'Justice', for example, is not just a word used to bracket certain events and situations together. Justice exists, it is a reality over and above any of the individual things that are said to be just. Indeed, the individual things are said to be 'just' because we have knowledge of justice itself.

These general realities he calls 'forms'. If we did not have knowledge of such a 'form' we would have no ability to put anything into a category. The 'form' of something is its essential feature, the thing that makes it what it is.

An example:

If I do not know the essence of dogginess, I will not be able to tell if the animal before me is a dog or a camel. Is it possible that I am looking at a tall dog with a hump, a long neck and bad breath? Equally, could that dachshund on a lead be a humpless, short-necked, particularly squat camel?

Description requires general terms, and general terms require an understanding of essences. Only with a prior appreciation of dogginess or camelality – if that is the correct term – can I hope to distinguish between then.

The ultimate 'form' for Plato (and the goal of the philosophical quest) is the 'Form of the Good'. An understanding of 'the good' enables all else to be valued. In other words, both in the doctrine of the forms, and in the analogy of the cave, Plato is describing the same process that concerns modern philosophers: the way in which we can relate our present experiences to reality itself. What Plato is saying is that our ordinary experience is no more than shadows, and that reality itself lies beyond them. We can have knowledge of the forms, because they are known by reason, whereas the most we can have of the individual things in the world of sensation is 'true belief', since it is always provisional and changing.

Plato's metaphysics is seen in his doctrine of forms. But how do we come by knowledge of them? In his dialogues, the protagonist (generally

...lenges someone to explain the meaning of a particular ..., by introducing examples by which to test out the ..., refines the concept. This implies that the use of reason ... give true knowledge of the forms. His justification for using ... .:thod of gaining knowledge (i.e. his epistemology) is that to kno.. or understand something is, in fact, to remember it. He believed that we all have knowledge of reality, but it is lost, cluttered by the changing experiences of the everyday world (as we sit in our cave, watching shadows). For Plato, we do not gather knowledge, we remember it. This recollection, he believed, was proof of immortality, for the soul must have been in the eternal realm of the forms before birth.

Aristotle (384 - 322BCE)

Aristotle rejected Plato's idea of forms that exist over and above particular things. He certainly believed that people needed to consider sorts of things, rather than each particular thing individually (try describing something without using general terms to indicate the kind of thing it is!), but he believed that the 'forms' were immanent in the particulars. In other words, I may look at a variety of things that are red, and say that what they have in common is redness. The quality 'redness' is actually part of my experience of those things. But what would it mean to have absolute redness; a redness that was not a red something or other? In Aristotle's philosophy, we do not go outside the world of experience in order to know the meaning of universal concepts, we simply apply them **within** experience.

This aims to overcome a basic problem with Plato's 'forms':

- I believe that this particular in front of me is a man.
- **Why?** Because I have knowledge of the Form of Man.
- **But**, given that all particulars are different – how do I know that this one belongs to the category 'man'? (It could be a robot, an ape, a pre-hominoid.)
- **Answer:** there must be a concept of 'man' over and above the Form and the particular, to which I refer when I claim that the one is a particular example of the other.
- **But** how do I know that **that** is in the right category? Only by having yet another concept of 'man' to which I can refer, and so on *ad infinitum!* (Which means that I can never know for sure that this is a man!)

This problem was recognised by Plato himself. It is generally known as the 'third-man argument'. By making the 'form' not something separate from the particulars, but simply a way of describing the particular sort of thing that these particulars are, this problem is avoided.

For Plato, knowledge had been limited to the world of forms, whereas the world known to the senses could yield, at best, only true belief. Eternal truths were detached from particular things. By contrast, having forms immanent within particulars, Aristotle claims that we can have true knowledge of the world of the senses.

There are many other important elements in Aristotle's metaphysics. One of them, his idea of causality, is of particular interest because it has implications both for metaphysics and also for the philosophy of religion. Aristotle argued that everything had four causes.

1. **Material** The material cause is the matter from which the thing is made.

2. **Formal** The formal cause is the kind of thing that something is (which follows from what we have been saying above about 'forms' in Plato and Aristotle).

3. **Efficient** The efficient cause is the agent that brings something about (the sense in which science would speak of a cause).

4. **Final** The final cause is the goal or purpose for which a thing is the way it is, and to which it is moving. This introduces the concept of the *telos*, or 'end'. If the world is rational, everything has its part to play, its purpose.

This had a considerable impact on the later philosophy of religion (as we shall see in chapter 2) and also on the 'natural law' approach to ethics (see chapter 5). It is also important because it acknowledges that the reality of a particular thing is not just a matter of its present substance and form, but it is related to agents in the past that have produced it and goals in the future to which it moves; both of which are part of its reality.

Metaphysics has to take account of the fact that there are individual things which need to be known and related to one another, but also (and implied every time we use language) there are universals, general concepts, a sense of the whole. Which of these should take priority? This dilemma is illustrated by two major metaphysical systems, those of Spinoza and Leibniz. Both are examples of rationalism (that one can come to a knowledge of reality by means of pure reason, as opposed to the empirical tradition, which based knowledge on the data of experience), and both follow from the tradition set by Descartes of trying to move from first principles to construct an overall view of the world.

Spinoza (1632-1677)

For Spinoza (and for Leibniz) the reality of the world, as known to reason, is very different from the appearance of the world as it is known to us through experience. Spinoza, a radical Jewish thinker, argued that God was the only absolute substance. His argument may be summarised as:

- If God is infinite, he must co-exist with everything.
- God must therefore be the only thing whose explanation lies within itself (all limited things can be caused by something external, but God can't, because there is nothing external to him).
- God is therefore the whole of the natural order.
- Although individual things may appear to be separate, they are in reality parts of a larger whole, which is God.
- The one true thing is the world as a whole.

In a most generalised way, we might say that the approach to appearance and reality taken by Spinoza is that a particular thing finds its reality only as part of a whole.

Leibniz (1646-1716)

Leibniz takes a view about particulars and wholes which is exactly the opposite of Spinoza. For Leibniz (following Descartes) the world is divided between mental things and physical or material things, and the essential difference between them is that physical things exist in space, but mental things do not. Now Leibniz saw that any material thing can be divided into its constituent parts, and these can be sub-divided. Ultimately, the world must therefore consist of an infinite number of individual things, which have no extension in space. But if they are indivisible, they cannot be physical and so must be mental in nature. He called them **monads**.

The argument might be expressed thus:

- Every complex thing can be divided into its constituent parts.
- These parts can be sub-divided again and again.
- Anything which has extension in space can be divided.
- Ultimately you arrive at an infinite number of monads, which occupy no space at all. They cannot be physical (otherwise they would be in space, and capable of being further divided), so they must be mental.

NOTE:

The view that the world is ultimately mental rather than physical is termed 'idealism', as opposed to 'materialism'.

How do these monads come together to form complex entities? Leibniz took the view that the monads could not influence one another directly. Rather, the world was arranged with a pre-established harmony, so that all the separate monads, each following its own course, actually managed to combine to give rise to the world we know, with its complex bodies.

IN OTHER WORDS:

- Which is more real – the whole or the parts of which it is comprised?
- Are there such things as justice or beauty (or any universal idea) or are there just individual things that we choose to describe as just or beautiful?
- In other words, how do you get beyond the things that appear to the senses? Is there a reality that lies beneath them, and, if so, can we ever get to understand it?

These are some of the basic questions for metaphysics.

Now we need to move on to two related areas – intuitive knowledge and the nature of language and its verification. In doing so we turn to some of the concerns that have been important for much twentieth century philosophy.

Intuitive knowledge

Intuition (direct knowledge, not the result of conscious reasoning or evidence) creates particular problems for those who base their knowledge of the world on sense experience. For example, I may feel, listening to a piece of music, that it 'says something' about life – something that is far beyond any analysis of the particular notes being played or the particles of pigment on canvas. I may experience 'ecstasy', in which I am quite outside myself, and momentarily, intuitively convinced of a reality which I subsequently fail to articulate precisely. A little alcoholic drink can have the same effect: an opening up of intuitive faculties, and a conviction that suddenly the whole world makes sense, that there is something of universal importance that one wants to say. But somehow, once sober again, it is difficult to put into words.

Some philosophers, whilst trying to accept that people do have ecstatic experiences, find that they do not readily move from them to posit any external reality. A J Ayer, interviewed for the *Observer* in 1980, was asked whether, when listening to music, there might be something other than what is scientifically verifiable; whether, for example, there could be a sense of ecstasy, and of something that was not fully explained. He replied:

> I don't particularly want to reduce aesthetic experiences to anything expressible in purely physical terms, but I don't think it's more mysterious than any other statement you might make about yourself. Clearly there is a problem about communicating feelings of any kind, since one has to take the other person's word for it. I can't, as it were, get inside your head and measure your ecstasy, but the statement that you feel ecstatic doesn't seem to me to create any particular problem. I know roughly what kind of feeling you're describing, what causes it, how it leads you to behave, when you are susceptible to it, how it fits in with the general pattern of your behaviour. Is the fact that you feel ecstatic more mysterious than that you feel bored, or any other sort of feeling?

[*The Observer*, 24th February 1980, p.35]

Notice what is happening in Ayer's answer. The question implied that there could be an intuition, in moments of ecstasy, which seemed to give awareness of something beyond scientific analysis. What Ayer does is to reduce it to the actual feeling - ecstasy – along with other feelings, like boredom. Having done that, the whole of the experience is one of understanding the internal workings of another person and his or her feelings. But what was being asked about was not ecstasy as 'feeling' but ecstasy as 'knowledge', and it is just this that Ayer does not accept.

NOTE:

For Plato, metaphysics is linked to morals. In *The Republic*, the Form of the Good is linked to practical moral problems. Only the person who understands the essential Form of Goodness is able to discern right from wrong. Metaphysics is not simply of academic interest, it shapes one's overall view of the world. Yet knowledge of the essential Form of the Good is not reducible to empirical statements about the bits and pieces of experience. In the cave analogy, the philosopher is for a moment blinded by the light as he steps out of the cave. Something is known intuitively, and only later, as the eyes adjust, is it actually perceived and known. Many things are known intuitively before they are understood, whether it be Einstein's intuition of relativity, or a mathematician who described a particular mathematical argument as 'elegant'. There may be a sense that something is right, even if, without further examination, it cannot be shown to be so.

Personal comment: It seems to me that a suitable analogy for the process of giving an empirical reduction of intuitive knowledge is that of taking the engine of a car to pieces to see how it works. It's fine as an academic exercise, but you can't drive the car while it is in a dismantled state! Intuition is the driving force of creative thinking.

—— Certainty, language and —— our view of the world

So far, in examining the quest for certainty we have looked at Descartes (who starts from himself as a thinking being) and the empiricists Hume and Ayer. We have seen the way in which Kant identified the contribution of the mind to our process of understanding the world.

We have also gone back to Plato and seen the way in which, for him, the world of appearances is but a shadow play, and that reality is in the world of 'forms'.

Probably the greatest influence in shaping modern life is science. We shall be looking at the philosophy of science in chapter 4, but for now it is necessary only to reflect on the fact that science is based on observation of the world, and that it uses empirical data from which to form hypotheses. With the obvious success of science, it was very tempting for philosophers to see science as in some way a paradigm for the way in which knowledge as a whole can be gained.

Science is based on observation. Each claim it makes is backed up with reference to data of some sort. Without data, there is no science. The language used by science is therefore justified with reference to external objects. It 'pictures' them. A statement is true if it corresponds to what has been observed, and false if it does not so correspond.

Logical Positivism

The 'Vienna Circle' was a group of philosophers who met in that city during the 1920s and 30s. In the broadest terms, they said:

- All metaphysics and theology were said to be literally 'meaningless' – since metaphysical and theological statement are neither a matter of logic (and therefore true by definition – *a priori*) nor are they provable by empirical evidence.
- Analytic propositions tell us nothing about the world. They are true by definition – and are therefore **tautologies**. They include the statements of logic and mathematics.
- Synthetic propositions are dependent upon evidence. Therefore there can be no necessary synthetic propositions.

Maurice Schlicke, one of the Vienna Circle, said that the meaning of a statement is its method of verification (this approach is generally known as **logical positivism**), and was promoted by the British philosopher A J Ayer (1910-89) in an important book entitled *Language, Truth and Logic* (1936). In that book he asks, What can philosophy do? His answer is that it certainly cannot tell us the nature of reality as such; in other words, it cannot provide us with metaphysics. If we want to know about reality we have to rely upon the evidence of our senses. Rather, philosophy has a single important task – analysis and clarification. Therefore, philosophy cannot give new information about anything. It looks at the words people use and analyses them, showing their logical implications. By doing so, philosophy clarifies muddled thought.

Ayer set out two forms of what can be called the verification principle. They are:

1. (a strong form) 'proposition is said to be verifiable in the strong sense if the term, if and only if its truth could be conclusively established in experience.'

2. (a weaker form) 'if it is possible for experience to render it probable' or 'some possible sense experience would be relevant to the determination of its truth or falsehood.'

Of course, other statements can have meaning, but Ayer is concerned with statements which have 'factual meaning'; in other words, if experience is not relevant to the truth or falsity of a statement, then that statement does not have factual meaning.

He argues that every genuine proposition, capable of being either true or false, should be either a tautology (in other words, true by definition) or else empirical hypothesis (something which makes a claim that can be verified by experience). For this reason, all metaphysics is regarded as nonsense, for it claims to make statements that are outside empirical verification, but also not true by definition.

An example of the strong form of this might be:

'There are three people in the next room.'
Meaning: If you go into the next room, you will see three people there.

Of course, it is not always possible to check information that easily. Where the evidence is not available, it was thought important to be able to specify what sort of evidence would count for or against a statement.

An example of the weaker form:

'Other planets within the universe supporting life.'
Meaning: If you were able to examine every planet in the universe, you would find others with life on them.

Although we have not been able to detect signs of carbon-based life like our own as yet, such a discovery would be able to show

---

that the statement is true. The statement is therefore 'meaningful'.

Statements are meaningless if there is nothing that would count for or against them being true. Now, on this basis, much of what passes for religious language, or aesthetics, or morality, would be categorised as 'meaningless', because none of these things can be specified in terms of concrete facts that can be checked by observation. It is a way of limiting the meaning of any statement to the scientific and empirical way of examining the world. If the only meaningful statement is one that makes an empirical proposition, there is really nothing more to say, although Ayer accepts that statements may be emotionally significant for him, even if they are not literally significant.

Logical positivism encounters two main problems:

1. How do I know that what I think I see is actually there? I could ask other people to look, checking if they see the same thing. But that would never actually prove that the object was there, for there is no way of getting beyond the sense experiences to the thing-in-itself. However many bits of evidence I get, I can never have absolute proof that there is an external thing being observed: we could all be mistaken.

2. How do we verify the statement 'The meaning of a statement is its method of verification?'
- Is it synthetic? If so what is the evidence for it? What evidence could count against it?
- Or is it analytic? If so then the word 'meaning' is logically the same as 'method of verification' and the theory doesn't say anything.

Showing the logical inconsistency within a theory is one way to discredit it, but it does not thereby render it of no further interest. The important thing about logical positivism is that it represents a particularly strong form of empiricism and a particularly narrow form of language. The service it has rendered philosophy is that, by showing what a wide range of propositions it considered 'meaningless', it required philosophers to revise and broaden their understanding of language, so that statements that are meaningless in simple 'picturing' terms take on meaning in other areas: expressing feelings; giving commands; stating preferences. This range of linguistic uses illustrates the flexibility of communication, and the need to get beyond simple empiricism.

On the other hand, the verification principle is a valuable check to make sure that statements about personal preferences or commands do not parade themselves as though they were straightforward empirical statements of fact.

Interestingly, towards the end of his life (as in the interview from which an extract was given earlier in this chapter), Ayer was to admit that his thought had developed since the time of writing *Language, Truth and Logic*, but it remains an important touchstone for a particular way of examining philosophy. Today, few would want to take on the bold claims of meaning and certainty of the Logical Positivists or Ayer, since philosophy has in general recognised the far more flexible nature of language and of the meaning of statements, but they came from a period when science and mathematics were seen to provide suitable images of clarity and precision, and therefore became models of an approach to which ordinary language was pressed to conform.

But where does that leave general statements about the world?

Language and perception

In what sense can a proposition be known to be true? In the Introduction we considered the way in which statements could be true by definition or true by experience. The former included statements of mathematics. Once the words were known, the truth or falsity of a statement followed automatically. But as we looked at statements based on experience, we found other problems. First of all, there is the uncertainty about any experience: it might always be mistaken or interpreted differently. Secondly, there is the way in which we have to use general words in order to describe particular things:

> **Example:**
>
> Imagine a situation in which there were no general words. How would you describe a tree without the words 'tree' or 'green' or 'tall' or 'thick', etc. Each of these words, unlike a proper name, has a meaning which can be applied to a variety of individual things; indeed, learning a language is about learning the whole range of general terms which we can put together in order to describe particular things.
>
> Do these general terms refer to things that exist, or are they merely 'names'. Does 'goodness' exist, or is it just a name for

certain kinds of things of which I approve? We saw this reflected in differences between Plato and Aristotle, and in the realist / nominalist debate.

In looking at logical positivism, we saw a philosophy that was based on the 'picturing' function of language. Statements only had meaning if they reflected evidence (or potential evidence) from the world of the senses. We may ask:

- How far can we trust our perception?
- Is perception the same as sense data?

It's all a matter of interpretation:

There are a number of examples of drawings that can be interpreted in a number of different ways. Here is a simple example:

Do you see the profiles of two people facing one another, or do you see an elegant chalice?

- Try switching your perception from one to the other – notice the mental effort involved.

- Is there any difference between the one and the other perception – difference, that is, in what is actually being seen?

Such visual games illustrate the ambiguity of all experience. As you make the mental effort to shift from one thing to the other, you are discovering the reality of 'experience as' – that all experience requires an element of interpretation, and that seeing a whole thing in one way will influence the perception of each individual part. Here is the dilemma facing any empirical method of verification for language:

- **If** all experience involved 'experiencing as'
- **And** if two people may therefore interpret the same data differently
- **How** do you decide between them or verify the truth of what they say?

NOTE:

It seems curious that, in logical positivism, philosophy was developing a narrow view of meaning (that of picturing items of sense data) at the very time when science was starting to realise that there can be two different and incompatible ways of viewing things, both of which can be considered correct. But we shall be considering this later, as part of the introduction to the philosophy of science in chapter 4.

The proof of the pudding ...

In examining matters of epistemology, it is tempting to take a common sense view: this or that must be right because it is the accepted and practical way of looking at things. The justification of a view being the fact that it is useful and solves problems.

There is a tradition of philosophy developed in America, and associated in particular with C S Peirce (1839-1914), William James (1842-1910) and John Dewey (1859-1952), known as **Pragmatism**. In the simplest of terms, pragmatism says:

- We act; we are not just spectators. The 'facts' about the world are shaped by our concerns, and what we hope to do.
- Beliefs should accord with known facts. But what should you do if the evidence is balanced between two theories?

Dewey emphasised the fact that we are not detached observers, but that we need to survive in the world. Knowledge is a problem-solving activity related to that need. Science is a dynamic process of gaining knowledge, helping us to gain mastery over our environment. Knowledge is therefore of practical importance.

A basic test to be applied to all statements is that of coherence. At any one time, we have a number of ways of seeing the world and working within it. A new theory, if it is to be accepted, needs to be compatible with existing accepted theories. Of course, this cannot be an absolute criterion of truth, or truth would be decided by committee and science would make no progress. Nevertheless, it is an important factor to be taken into account. This issue of testing out new views will be considered again under the Philosophy of Science.

Knowledge and language

As far as philosophers in the Anglo-American tradition were concerned (see chapter 7 for the different approach taken by Continental philosophy), for much of the twentieth century, philosophy was dominated by the discussion of language. Indeed, there was a feeling that this was all that philosophy was about, everything else being sorted out by sciences or politics or sociology. Philosophy, rather than having any specific content, was an activity, and that activity was to do with the sorting out of words and their meaning. Philosophy has sometimes been given a role rather like that of an indigestion tablet – something necessary in order to purify the system and enable comfort and efficiency to return. So philosophy would help every other subject, by clearing away its confusions about language.

We saw earlier that the logical positivists argued that the meaning of a statement was given as its method of verification. This view attempted to purge language of all that could not be reduced to sense experience. Metaphysics was out, and ethics was little more than the expression of a preference for certain things. By the 1950s, this view of language was becoming broader. Wittgenstein (who, in the earlier phase of his work had espoused this radically reductionist approach to language) broadened his view, and accepted that language could take on different functions, of which straight description of phenomena was only one. This allowed more flexibility, and recognised that the expression of values and emotions, the giving of orders and making of requests, were all valid uses of language. They were all different 'language games'.

At this point, philosophers seemed to be catching up with common sense, and abandoning the purity of the unchallengeable statement as the goal of meaning. But, as we saw in the interview with Ayer, philosophers may still have trouble in coming to terms with those experiences which purport to give intuition about reality, but which are not reducible to empirical data.

In chapter 5 we shall be examining different tasks that language can perform in the field of ethics. What we need to recognise at this point is that language is not simple and transparent. The words we use, and the meaning we give to our statements, reflect our metaphysics, and are justified in terms of our epistemology.

IN OTHER WORDS:

- People (hopefully) think before they speak.
- They may also perceive before they think.

Therefore:

- What they say reflects the nature of thought and of perception.
- Language is therefore only as simple and straightforward as the thought and perception that produced it.

Add intuition, emotion and the general confusions of human life, and the resulting language is very complex indeed.

- It may perform many different functions.
- It may play many different games.
- We may not even be aware of the implications of what we are saying, which is to return to Plato, who in his dialogues portrays Socrates as a man who is constantly asking people what they mean, and thereby exposing their confusions and opening up the way to greater clarity;
- without language we cannot have metaphysics or epistemology: indeed, we cannot have philosophy, civilisation, culture or other distinctively human features of life.

—————— Some conclusions ——————

Knowing is a creative activity, and always involves an element of interpretation. We know nothing with absolute certainty, except those things which are true by definition. On the other hand – as we saw Russell doing as he contemplated his desk – we can gradually build up a degree of reasonable certainty.

What we claim to know for certain, depends on what we count as a true sentence. In his book *Tractatus*, Wittgenstein started with the bold statement 'The world is everything that is the case.' In this, he took the general idea of language as picturing the external world, and that it is true or false depending on whether or not it gives an accurate picture. This allows a degree of certainty, but also excludes much ordinary language from having any meaning – for not all language pictures the world.

Wittgenstein admitted (section 5.632) that 'The subject does not belong to the world; rather it is a limit of the world.' This means that the self remains unknown. Anything I say about my body, about my interests or activities, becomes something external to myself, a sign of my action in the world, but not me as I am in myself. If this is threatening, there is comfort to be had in the same argument (section 6.4311) 'Death is not an event in life: we do not live to experience death.' At the end of the book (section 7) he says 'What we cannot speak about we must consign to silence.' Language pictures reality, and is true where it corresponds to it. But the self, and death, are not part of that world, and cannot be approached using that narrow definition of language.

Early in this chapter we looked at Descartes and his systematic doubt – his determination to set aside all previously held opinions and accept only what he could see clearly and distinctly to be true. In practice, however, there needs to come some point at which there seems no need to maintain total scepticism. Descartes himself saw no reason to believe that the created order should deceive us – and therefore he could accept as true what he perceived clearly to be so. Russell (in *The Problem of Philosophy*) came to accept the reality of the external object – his table – on the grounds that it was seen by a number of different people at the same time, and that its shared experience was a valid basis for asserting the objectivity of the table. Perhaps, after all, there is scope for common sense in philosophy!

In terms of epistemology, we saw that the American pragmatist tradition looked to accept those ideas and theories that were most productive, most useful, recognising that human beings do not simply contemplate the world but are – at least on a temporary basis – part of it.

A similar test might be applied to metaphysics in general. Consider the practical and emotional implications of Plato's theory of the forms. It is possible for a Platonic approach to lead to a view that the present world as encountered by the senses is inferior, partial, lacking in inherent value. The philosopher is constantly looking beyond what is present, out to another, ideal world. Justice, love, beauty, truth – if these are encountered at all in the present world they are but pale reflections of their abstract, ideal counterparts.

The religious implications of this (and, indeed, the influence of Plato on the development of the Christian religion) is considerable. Reality, from this perspective, is located outside the present known world, not within it.

A PERSONAL POSTSCRIPT:

A fundamental problem within Western philosophy has been the view that 'self' and 'world' are separate things, with the one trying to find out if the other is actually there. In reality, what we call 'self' is a temporary and changing part of what we call 'world'. There are not two separate realities, but one.

Experience is not an object (sense data do not exist); it is the term we use for the relationship that all sentient beings have with the rest of the world. It is both physical and mental; it is sharing not gathering; it is always changing, not fixed. Philosophy needs to take into account this fundamental unity and interactive nature of life.

2

THE PHILOSOPHY OF RELIGION

In Western thought, the philosophy of religion is concerned with:

- Religious language: what it means, what it does and whether it can be shown to be true or false.
- Metaphysical claims: (e.g. that God exists) the nature of the arguments by which such claims are defended, and the basis upon which those claims can be shown to be true or false.

Three features of religion are of particular interest:

- Religious experience: what it is, and what sort of knowledge it can yield.
- Miracles: in particular, whether there can ever be sufficient evidence to prove that a miracle has taken place.
- The problem of evil: whether belief in a God is compatible with the existence of suffering and evil in the world.

The nature and status of religious language

If you describe a religious event or organisation, the language you use need not be especially religious. Consider the following:

> The Pope is the Bishop of Rome.
> The Jewish religion forbids the eating of pork.

The first of these is true by definition, since 'The Pope' is a title used for the Bishop of Rome. The second can be shown to be true by looking at the Jewish scriptures. (It would not be made invalid by evidence that a non-practising Jew had been seen eating a bacon sandwich, for the moral and religious rules remain true, even if they are broken.

Provided that the terms are understood, and there is evidence to back up any claims, there is, in general, no problem with this kind of **descriptive language**, as far as religion is concerned. Religious people themselves use language in a variety of ways. They may pray, give thanks, hold moral discussions, make statements about their beliefs. These again, provided that the terms are understood, present no particular philosophical problems.

Religious beliefs

The main area in which religious language causes philosophical problems is in the area of metaphysics – statements of belief about that which is beyond the ordinary experienced world of space and time. As we saw in chapter 1, some philosophers might want to dismiss metaphysics as meaningless, and along with it they would therefore discard most statements of religious belief.

What is distinctive about religious questions and beliefs?

How? and Why?

One way of expressing a distinctive flavour of religious language is to highlight the difference between 'How?' questions and 'Why?' questions. Science answers 'How?' questions by explaining how individual parts of the world relate to one another. But religion asks 'Why?'; not 'How does the world work?' but 'Why is there a world at all?'

A 'Why?' question asks about meaning and purpose. It cannot be answered in terms of empirical facts alone. This is illustrated by a story by John Wisdom (a version of which is set out in *New Essays in Philosophical Theology* by Anthony Flew):

Two explorers come across a clearing in the jungle. It contains a mixture of weeds and flowers. One claims that there must be a gardener who comes to tend the clearing. The other denies it. They sit and wait, but no gardener appears, however many ways they try to detect him.

One continues to deny that there is a gardener. The other says that there is gardener: one who is invisible and undetectable. But – and this is the central point of the argument – how do you distinguish an invisible gardener whose activity is open to question, from the idea that there is no gardener at all?

As originally presented, this story was used to show that a good idea could die the death of a thousand qualifications. In other words, when all obvious qualities that the gardener might have are eliminated, nothing of any significance remains. But the story also illustrates the idea of a 'blik' – a particular 'view' of things. In the story, the same evidence is available to the two explorers, but they choose to interpret it differently. We have our own particular 'blik' and interpret everything in the light of it. It can be argued that religious belief is just one such 'blik'; one way of organising our experience of the world. As such it is no more or less true than anyone else's blik, and every arguments ends with someone saying, 'Well, if that's the way you want to see it...'.

The personal aspects of language

I T Ramsey, in *Religious Language* (SCM Press, 1957), pointed out that there were elements of both discernment and commitment in religious statements. They were not simply detached comments, but indicated a whole attitude and determination to follow a corresponding way of life. Thus, although they include facts, they are far more complex than that. He makes the essential point that the word 'God' is used to describe a reality about which the believer wishes to communicate. It is not simply a matter of speculation.

We may therefore distinguish between the philosopher who examines an argument for the existence of God in an objective and disinterested way, and the religious believer who uses 'God' to express a sense of direction, purpose, meaning which comes through religious and moral experience.

Arguments for the existence of God can be seen as:

1. discussions of something which may or may not exist;
2. indications of what it is a religious believer is talking about when he or she speaks of 'God'.

Ramsey uses the terms **models** and **qualifiers** to explain the way in which religious language differs from ordinary empirical language. A 'model' is like an analogy – an image that helps a person to articulate that which is rather different from anything else. For example, if God is called a 'designer', it does not imply that the religious believer has some personal knowledge of a process of design carried out by God, simply that the image of someone who designs is close to his or her experience of God. On the other hand, having offered the 'model' it is then important for the religious believer to offer a 'qualifier' – God is an 'infinite' this, or a 'perfect' that – the model is therefore qualified, so that it is not mistakenly taken in a literal way.

IN OTHER WORDS:

- Religious language is sometimes simply descriptive (e.g. of religious activities).
- When it expresses beliefs it may be:

  – a particular way of looking at the world (a 'blik);

  – based on personal commitment (not simply a matter of speculation).

- Since it is not simply a statement of fact, to be checked against evidence, such religious language is 'meaningless' from the point of view of logical positivism (see above p.36).

—————— Does God exist? ——————

We shall look at some traditional arguments for the existence of God, and the problems they raise. But first we need to have some working idea of what is meant by the word 'God'.

Since we are concerned with Western philosophy, the relevant concepts have come from the Western theistic religions – Judaism, Christianity and Islam. For these, God may be said to be a supreme being, infinite, spiritual and personal, creator of the world. He is generally described as all-powerful (having created the world out of nothing, he can do anything he wishes) and all-loving (in a personal caring relationship with individual believers). Although pictured in human form, he is believed to be beyond literal description (and is thus not strictly male, although 'he' is generally depicted as such).

Some terms:

- Belief in the existence of God is **theism.**
- The conviction that no such being exists is **atheism.**
- The view that there is no conclusive evidence to decide whether God exists or not is **agnosticism.**
- An identification of God with the physical universe is **pantheism.**
- The belief that God is within everything (but not simply identified with the physical universe) is **panentheism.** (Although this term is used by some theologians, most interpretations of theism include the idea of God being 'within'; indeed, if he is infinite, there is nothing which is external to him.)
- The idea of an external designer God who created the world, but is not immanent within it, is **deism.**

In his *Critique of Pure Reason* (section A 590-591), Kant argued that there could be only three types of argument for the existence of God: 1) based on reason alone, 2) based on the general fact of the existence of the world, and 3) based on particular features of the world. They are called the **ontological, cosmological** and **teleological** arguments. He offered a critique of all three, and introduced a fourth one: the moral argument.

The ontological argument

The ontological argument for the existence of God is not based on observation of the world, or on any form of external evidence, but simply on a particular definition of the meaning of 'God'. In other words, it says:

If you understand what God is, you understand that he must exist.

This argument is of particular interest to philosophers, because it raises questions about language and about metaphysics which apply to issues other than religious belief.

The argument was set out by Anselm (1033-1109), Archbishop of Canterbury, in the opening chapters of his *Proslogion*. He makes it clear that he is not putting forward this argument in order to be able to believe in God, but that his belief leads him to understand God's existence in this particular way – a way which leads him to the conclusion that God **must** exist.

Religious experience leads him to speak of God as, *aliquid quo nihil maius cogitari possit* – 'the most real being, than which nothing greater can be thought'. [This does **not** mean something that just happens to be physically bigger, or better, than anything else – it is the idea of 'perfection', or 'the absolute', the most real thing (*ens reallissimum*).]

In the second chapter of *Proslogion*, the argument is presented in this way:

> Now we believe that thou are a being than which none greater can be thought. Or can it be that there is no such being, since 'the fool hath said in his heart, "There is no God"'? [Psalm 14:1; 53:1] But when this same fool hears what I am saying – 'A being than which none greater can be thought' – he understands what he hears, and what he understands is in his understanding, even if he does not understand that it exists. For it is one thing for an object to be in the understanding, and another thing to understand that it exists ... But clearly that than which a greater cannot be thought cannot exist in the understanding alone. For if it is actually in the understanding alone, it can be thought of as existing also in reality, and this is greater. Therefore, if that than which a greater cannot be thought is in the understanding alone, this same thing than which a greater cannot be thought is that than which a greater can be thought. But obviously this is impossible. Without doubt, therefore, there exists, both in the understanding and in reality, something than which a greater cannot be thought.

In other words, something is greater if it exists than if it doesn't. If God is the greatest thing imaginable, he must exist. I may paint an imaginary masterpiece – but that only means I imagine that I paint a masterpiece. In fact, since it does not exist, it is no better than my actually existing 'inferior' paintings. A real masterpiece must always be better than an imaginary one!

One of the clearest criticisms of this argument was made by Kant (in his *Critique of Pure Reason*) in response to Descartes, who had maintained, in his version of the argument, that it was impossible to have a triangle without having its three sides and angles, and in the same way it was impossible to have God without having necessary existence. Kant's argument may be set out like this:

- **If** you have a triangle

- **Then** it must have three angles

(i.e. a triangle without three angles is a contradiction)

- **But** if you do not have the triangle, you do not have its three angles or sides either.

In the same way, Kant argued:

- **If** you accept God, it is logical to accept his necessary existence
- **But** you do not have to accept God.

To appreciate the force of Kant's argument, it is important to remember that he divided all statements into two categories – *analytic* and *synthetic* (see Introduction p7):

- **analytic statements** are true by definition;
- **synthetic statements** can only be proved true or false with reference to experience.

For Kant, statements about existence are synthetic; definitions are analytic. Therefore, the angles and sides of a triangle are necessary because they are part of the definition of a triangle. But that says nothing about the **actual** existence of a triangle – necessity (for Kant) is not a feature of the world, but only of logic and definition.

Kant gives another way of expressing the same idea. He says that **existence is not a predicate**. In other words, if you describe something completely, you add nothing to that description by then saying 'and it has existence'. Existence is not an extra quality – it is just a way of saying that there is the thing itself, with all the qualities already given.

Norman Malcolm (in *Philosophical Review* January, 1960) pointed out that Kant's criticism failed in an important respect. You can either have a triangle or not, but (on Anselm's definition) you simply cannot have no God, so the two situations are not exactly parallel.

For Anselm, then, 'God' is a unique concept. This was something that he had to clarify early on, in the light of criticism from Gaunilo, a fellow monk, who raised the idea of the perfect island, claiming that, if Anselm's argument were true, then the perfect island would also have to exist. Anselm rejected this. An island is a limited thing, and you can always imagine better and better islands. But he holds that 'a being than which a greater cannot be thought' is unique. If it could be thought of as nonexistent, it could also be thought of as having a beginning and an end, but then it would not be the greatest that can be thought.

This is another version of the argumen that he had already introduced in chapter 3 of the *Proslogion*:

> Something which cannot be thought of as not existing... is greater than that which *can* be thought of as not existing. Thus, if that than which a greater cannot be thought can be thought of as not existing, this very thing than which a greater cannot be thought is *not* that than which a greater cannot be thought. But this is contradictory. So, then, there truly is a being than which a greater cannot be thought – so truly that it cannot even be thought of as not existing.

In other words, Anselm claims that existence is a **necessary** part of the idea of God. But he goes one step further. In chapter 4 of *Proslogion*, he asks how the fool can still claim that God does not exist, and concludes:

> For we think of a thing, in one sense, when we think of the word that signifies it, and in another sense, when we understand the very thing itself. Thus in the first sense God can be thought of as nonexistent, but in the second sense this is quite impossible. For no one who understands what God is can think that God does not exist ... For God is that than which a greater cannot be thought, and whoever understands this rightly must understand that he exists in a way that he cannot be nonexistent even in thought. He, therefore, who understands that God thus exists cannot think of him as nonexistent.

For Anselm, God is not thought of as an object alongside others; the word 'God' is not used as a name for something. Indeed, if God were an object, then the worship of him would be idolatry. **So what did Anselm understand by speaking of God as 'that than which none greater can be thought'?**

In another work, *Monologion*, he spoke of degrees of goodness and perfection in the world, and that there must be something that constitutes perfect goodness, which he calls 'God', which causes goodness in all else. This idea of the degrees of perfection was not new. Aristotle had used this idea in *De Philosophia*, and it is also closely related to Plato's idea of Forms. Anselm's idea of God comes close to Plato's Form of the Good.

There are several philosophical points to be explored here. (Which is why this argument has been set out at greater length than others in this book.) Let us clarify this argument by taking a silly example:

You have a classroom full of pupils, and told that they are 'Class 1A'.

• Where is the 'class'?

• You ask each of the pupils in turn, but each gives only his or her name.

• You conclude that the 'Class 1A' does not exist.

This is what is called a **category mistake**. Class 1A is real, and comprises the pupils – but there does not exist anything that is 'Class 1A', which is not also something else, namely a particular pupil. (We shall come up against category mistakes again in Ryle's concept of mind in chapter 3.)

Although it is rather different, you might think of 'the perfect pupil' in the same way. However good a particular pupil might be, you could always imagine one that was just a little better. 'The perfect pupil' exists in a different category from individual pupils. The perfect pupil does not appear in the class, because (however good individual pupils might be) you can always imagine a better one. But if you had no idea of what a perfect pupil might be like, there would be no way of judging between one pupil and another. 'The perfect pupil' can be seen as a necessary concept in order to make any sense of putting the pupils in some sort of rank order.

Some might see the putting of pupils in order of merit as politically incorrect, arguing that the idea of 'the perfect pupil' is dangerous since all are equally good, each in his or her own way! But if you remove ideals, how do you judge anything good or bad? Perhaps 'that than which a greater cannot be thought' is an absolute which enables us to compare and give value to things.

The class of pupils can illustrate a second point: **A comparative or superlative term is not a quality, but simply shows a relationship.**

To say that a pupil is the tallest in the class is not a fixed quality that a particular pupil has, but is simply a way of comparing sizes. You do not eliminate the idea of 'the tallest pupil' by amputation – the amputee might be demoted, but immediately there would be some other pupil who qualified as 'the tallest'. What is more, that pupil would not have grown at all since he or she was second tallest! There is no additional height, just a new relationship. So:

• 'the perfect ...' is in a different category from individual things;

• 'the perfect ...' is not simply the top of a series of individual things.

God, for Anselm, is not an object, and therefore does not 'exist' in the way that other objects exist. Anselm's idea of God springs from his awareness of degrees of goodness in the world.

This is like the idea of Plato's 'cave', which we considered in the last chapter. What was taken for reality by those in the cave was in fact only a set of shadows, cast because of light coming from behind them. The wise man, although not able to see the source of the light directly, yet knows that it is there beyond the entrance to the cave – the Form of the Good.

Something of the same can be said of this argument. The 'greatest thing' for Anselm is an intuition – something seen as necessary once lesser values are recognised as being a shadow of something greater.

This approach to the ontological argument is taken by Iris Murdoch in her book *Metaphysics as a Guide to Morals*. She holds that an argument about necessary existence can only be taken in the context of this Platonic view of degrees of reality. She points out that what the proof does is not simply logical, but something that points to a spiritual reality that transcends any limited idea of God. It is also something that goes beyond individual religions:

> 'An ultimate religious 'belief' must be that even if all 'religions' were to blow away like mist, the necessity of virtue and the reality of the good would remain. This is what the Ontological Proof tries to 'prove' in terms of a unique formulation.' (*op cit* p.427)

And this, she claims, is a necessary part of our understanding of life:

> 'What is perfect must exist, that is, what we think of as goodness and perfection, the 'object' of our best thoughts, must be something real, indeed especially and most real, not as contingent accidental reality but as something fundamental, essential and necessary. What is experienced as most real in our lives is connected with a value which points further on. Our consciousness of failure is a source of knowledge. We are constantly in the process of recognising the falseness of our 'goods', and the unimportance of what we deem important. Great art teaches a sense of reality, so does ordinary living and loving.' (p.430)

IN OTHER WORDS:

- If we simply think of the ontological argument in terms of 'existence is a predicate,' then Kant was probably right, and Anselm wrong – for to say that something 'exists' is quite different from anything else that can be said about it.

- Anselm's argument also shows that some idea of 'the greatest that can be thought' is a necessary part of the way we thing, since, every time we ascribe value to something, we do so on the basis of an intuition of that which has supreme value.

- At its heart, the ontological argument is about how we relate the ordinary conditioned and limited things we experience to the idea of the perfect, the absolute and the unconditioned – and that, as we saw in the last chapter, is a key question for philosophy.

—— The cosmological arguments ——

Thomas Aquinas (1225-74) presented **Five Ways** in which he believed the existence of God could be shown. They are:

1. The argument from an unmoved mover.
2. The argument from an uncaused cause.
3. The argument from possibility and necessity.
4. The argument from degrees of quality.
5. The argument from design.

The fourth of these has already been considered, for a version of it came in Anselm's *Monologion*. The last will be examined in the next section. For now, therefore we need to look at the first three, which are generally termed 'cosmological arguments'.

The ontological argument was based on logic – on the apparent impossibility of really understanding the meaning of 'that than which no greater can be conceived', whilst at the same time believing that such a being did not exist.

Cosmological arguments are based on the observation of the world. They originate in the thinking of Aristotle, whom Aquinas regarded as the principal philosopher. The first may be presented like this:

- Everything that moves is moved by something.
- That mover is in turn moved by something else again.
- **But** this chain of movers cannot be infinite, or movement would not

have started in the first place.

- **Therefore** there must be an unmoved mover, causing movement in everything, without itself actually being moved.
- This unmoved mover is what people understand by 'God'.

The second argument has the same structure:

- Everything has a cause.
- Every cause itself has a cause.
- **But**, you cannot have an infinite number of causes.
- **Therefore** there must be an uncaused cause, which causes everything to happen without itself being caused by anything else.
- Such an uncaused cause is what people understand by 'God'.

The third argument follows from the first two:

- Individual things come into existence and later cease to exist.
- **Therefore** at one time none of them was in existence.
- **But** something comes into existence only as a result of something else that already exists.
- **Therefore** there must be a being whose existence is necessary – 'God'.

One possible objection to these arguments is to say that you might indeed have an infinite number of causes or movers. Instead of stretching back into the past in a straight line, the series of causes could be circular, or looped in a figure of eight, so that you never get to a first cause, and everything is quite adequately explained by its immediate causes. This image of circularity does not really help us to understand the force of Aquinas' argument, for it is unlikely that he was thinking of a series of causes (or movers) stretching into the past. His argument actually suggests a hierarchy of causes here and now. Every individual thing has its cause: Why should the whole world not have a cause beyond itself? You could therefore argue that within a circular series of causes, each individual cause would be caused by its neighbour, but what then is the cause of the whole circle of causes? If the world itself had such a cause, that cause too would require a cause, for it would have become part of the known world. The philosopher Kant argued that causality is one of the ways in which our minds sort out the world – we impose causality upon our experience. If Kant is right, then an uncaused cause is a mental impossibility.

A rather different objection came from Hume. In the last chapter we noted the way in which he based all knowledge on the observation of the world. Something is said to be a cause because it is seen to occur just before the thing that is called its effect. That depends on the observation of cause and effect as two separate things. **But**, in the case of the world as a whole, you have a unique effect, and therefore cannot observe its cause. You cannot get 'outside' the world to see both the world and its cause, and thus establish the relationship between them. If, with Hume, you consider sense impressions as the basis of all knowledge, then the cosmological proofs cannot be accepted as giving proof of the existence of a God outside the world of observation.

Perhaps this gives a clue to a different way of approaching these cosmological arguments. If we follow them in a literal and logical way, they do not prove that there is an uncaused cause or unmoved mover. But they show how a religious person may use the idea of movement or cause to point to the way in which he or she sees God – as a being that in some way stands behind yet causes or moves everything; something beyond and yet involved with everything.

The argument from design

Although Aquinas has a form of this argument, the clearest example of it is given by William Paley (1743-1805). He argues that, if he were to find a watch lying on the ground, he would assume that it was the product of a designer, for, unlike a stone, he would see at once that it was made up of many different parts worked together in order to produce movement, and that, if any one part were ordered differently, then the whole thing would not work.

In the same way he argued that the world is like a machine, each part of it designed so that it takes its place within the whole. If the world is so designed, it must have a designer, which is God.

This argument, reflecting the sense of wonder at nature, was most seriously challenged by the theory of evolution. Darwin's 'natural selection' provided an alternative explanation for design, and one that did not require the aid of any external designer. At once, it became possible to see the world not as a machine, but as a process of struggle and death in which the fittest were able to breed and pass their genes on to the next generation, thus influencing the very gradual development of the species. Adaptation in order to survive became the key to development of the most elaborate of forms, which previously would have been described as an almost miraculous work of a designer God.

Actually, the challenge of natural selection was anticipated in the work of Hume, who set out a criticism of the design argument some twenty three years before Paley wrote his version of it. He argued that in a finite world and given infinite time, any combination of things can occur. Those that work together harmoniously can continue, those that do not will fail. Therefore all that we observe must represent that which works.

For reflection:

All the parts of your body work together. If you had no lungs, you could not breathe, and the rest of your body would fail for lack of oxygen. Does this imply a careful designer? You could argue that all creatures who require oxygen from the air but are born without lungs are likely to die very quickly. Such creatures cannot exist. Only those with the means of getting the oxygen will exist. This works by simple logic, and does not even require natural selection.

- Everything is as it is.
- If anything were different, everything would be different.
- Everything contributes to everything else.
- If everything else were different, everything would contribute differently.
- Therefore the argument from design works only in retrospect.

The moral argument

Kant believed that the cosmological arguments could never prove the existence of God, but that, by getting rid of those arguments, he could make way for an understanding of God based on faith, rather than reason. He did this by examining the idea of moral experience, and in particular the ideas of virtue and happiness. In an ideal world they should follow one another – that, if there is a highest good, and if a person is morally inclined to pursue it, then doing what is right (virtue) should ultimately lead to happiness. But clearly, there is no evidence that virtue will lead to happiness. Why then should anyone be moral?

Kant started from the fact that people do have a sense of moral obligation: a feeling that something is right and must be done, no matter what the consequences. He called this sense of moral obligation the **categorical imperative**, to distinguish it from a **hypothetical imperative** (which says, 'if you want to achieve this, then you must do that').

In *The Critique of Practical Reason* Kant starts to explore the presuppositions of the categorical imperative. What do I actually believe about life if I respond to the absolute moral demand? (Not, what must I rationally accept before I agree with a moral proposal, but what do I actually feel to be true, rationally or otherwise, in the moment when I respond to the moral imperative?) He presented the idea that three things – God, freedom and immortality – were *postulates* of the practical reason. This meant that the experience of morality implied that you were free to act (even if someone observing you claimed that you were not), that you would eventually achieve the result you wanted (even if you would not do so in this life, as when someone sacrificed his or her own life), and that, for any of this to be possible, there had to be some overall ordering principle, which might be called 'God'.

In other words, Kant is saying that you cannot prove the existence of God, but, if you know what it is to feel obliged to act morally, you sense what that belief is really about. For Kant, this was to be the way by which speculative metaphysics (which could never give knowledge of God) would give way to practical certainty, based on actual moral experience.

The way in which Kant saw the world obliged him to go beyond the traditional arguments for the existence of God. After all, if the idea of causality is imposed on external reality by our own minds, how can it become the basis for a proof for the existence of God? We can only know things as they appear to us, not as they are in themselves.

- **If** we contribute space, time and causality to our understanding of the world,
- **Then** to argue from these to something outside the world is impossible.
- God, freedom and immortality are therefore not **in** the world that we experience, but have to do with **the way in which** we experience the world.
- In other words, God is a 'regulative' concept (part of our way of understanding) not a 'constitutive' concept (one of the things out there to be discovered).

In many ways, far from demolishing the traditional proofs, Kant tends to strengthen them – for, taken literally, they do not work, but, taken symbolically, they point beyond experience to something absolute – and this is just what Kant is trying to express in his 'regulative' idea.

In considering all the arguments about the existence of God, it might be worth keeping the whole exercise in perspective by reminding ourselves that the sort of 'God' whose existence might or might not be the case is not what many people term 'God' anyway. Of course, this was the basis of the ontological argument, but it is relevant to consider it in the context of a modern theologian, Paul Tillich. In his *Systematic Theology* (Vol. I p.262), he says:

> '... the question of the existence of God can be neither asked nor answered. If asked, it is a question about that which by its very nature is above existence, and therefore the answer – whether negative or affirmative – implicitly denies the nature of God. It is as atheistic to affirm the existence of God as to deny it. God is being-itself, not a being.'

This reinforces what has been implied throughout the ontological and cosmological arguments; that what is being claimed is not the existence of one entity alongside others, but a fundamental way of regarding the whole universe. It is about the structures of being-itself (to use Tillich's term), not the possible existence of a being.

IN OTHER WORDS:

- The cosmological and design arguments suggest that there are features of the world which lead the mind to that which goes beyond experience: What is the cause of everything? Why is the world as it is?

- The moral argument suggests that we all have an intuition of God (along with freedom and immortality) every time we experience a sense of absolute moral obligation.

- Even if these arguments are not conclusive, they do indicate the sort of thing a religious person is thinking about when he or she uses the word 'God'.

The meaning of 'God'

The arguments set out above presuppose a generally accepted idea of what 'God' means. Earlier we looked at a basic idea of 'God', but let us now take it a little further.

The most stringent test of the meaning of a statement is that given by logical positivism (see p36). Under this set of rules, a statement has a meaning if it pictures something that can be verified by sense experience. If no evidence is relevant to its truth, a statement is meaningless.

When we turn to language about God, such verification is not possible. Most definitions of 'God' are such as to preclude any explanation in terms of what can be directly experienced. This would lead a strict logical positivist to say that statements about God are meaningless.

The broader perspective sees each form of language in terms of its function. Religious language finds its meaning in terms of what it does. So, for example, 'God' (for a religious believer) is not simply the name of some external object, about whose existence there could be a debate. Such a 'God' would not be adequate religiously, and to prove his existence would not significantly contribute to religious debate. In other words:

- **If** you prove that God 'exists' in a way that would satisfy a logical positivist (i.e. testable by empirical evidence),
- **Then** 'God' becomes part of the world,
- **So** he is no longer 'God'.

It is important thing to keep this in mind, because it might be possible to see the arguments for the existence of God as either succeeding or failing to give definitive proof of the objective existence of an entity called 'God'. This is simplistic, and is only part of the issue. More important is to ask what part such arguments play in the religious perception of the believer.

Generally speaking, the arguments show the sort of place that the idea of God has in terms of the perception of the world – to say that he is the uncaused cause, or the designer of the world, is to locate God in the realm of overall meaning and purpose. Convictions of that are a 'blik' that is unlikely to be changed by (but could be strengthened by) the traditional arguments.

'Being-itself' and 'ultimate concern'

Let us return for a moment to the theologian Paul Tillich, whose idea of 'being-itself' was mentioned above. Tillich insisted that religious ideas could only be expressed by way of symbols. A symbol is something that conveys the power and meaning of the thing it symbolises, in contrast to a sign, which is merely conventional. He argued that the religious experience has two elements; the material basis (the actual thing seen, which could be analysed by science) and the sense of ultimate value and power which it conveys, and which makes it 'religious'. For him there were two essential features of this:

1. That God is 'being-itself' rather than a being. In other words, an experience of God is not an experience of something that just happens to be there, an object among others, but is an experience of life itself, of being-itself, an experience which then gives meaning to everything else.

2. That God is 'ultimate concern'. This implied that 'God' could not be thought of in a detached and impartial way. For the religious believer, God demands total attention and commitment, covering all partial concerns, all other aspects of life. This sense of God as the most important thing in life, is seen in the nature of religious experience.

THEREFORE:

- You cannot describe God literally (all language must be symbolic).
- God is not a being among others, he is 'being-itself'.
- God is the name for what the religious person encounters in a way that is personal and demanding, not casual and detached.

Language about 'God' need not be religious. You can have a statement about the structure of the universe which includes the idea of God, but that does not make it religious. In order for something to be religious, it has to use religious language in a way that reflects religious experience and/or religious practice. There are two other distinctive features of religious language:

1. The Jewish philosopher Martin Buber introduced the important distinction between 'I-Thou' and 'I-It' language. 'I-Thou' language is personal, whilst 'I-It' is impersonal. Religious language is about an I addressing a Thou, not speculating about an It.

2. The distinction is often made between 'believing that' and 'believing in'. You believe **that** something is the case if you rationally hold it to be so. On the other hand, it may be of no personal interest to you at all. You believe **in** something if you are personally committed to it. The essential limitation of the arguments for the existence of God is that they attempt to show that it is reasonable to believe **that God exists**, rather than to show why people **believe in God**.

But in order to appreciate religious language, we need to reflect on at least some aspects of religious experience.

———— Religious experience ————

Philosophy of religion would be quite impossible without religion. If nobody had religious experiences, there would be no basis for the idea of a 'God'. So what is it that makes an experience religious?

The nineteenth century religious writer Schleiermacher described religious awareness in terms of a 'feeling of dependence', and of seeing finite things in and through the infinite. This was rather like mystical experience – a sudden awareness of a wider dimension, which throws new light on the ordinary world around us. What Schleiermacher was trying to express was that religion was not a matter of dogma or logic, but was based on a direct experience of oneself as being small and limited, against the background of the eternal. It was also an identification of the self with the whole: a sense of belonging to the whole world. Feelings like that are destroyed by logic; they are not the result of reasoning but of intuition.

Rudolph Otto, in his famous book *The Idea of the Holy* (1917), argued that the religious experience was essentially about the Mysterium Tremendum – something totally other, unknowable; something that is awesome in its dimensions and power; something which is also attractive and fascinating. He outlined a whole range of feelings ('creeping flesh'; the fear of ghosts; the sense of something that is uncanny, weird or eerie) to illustrate that this encounter is with something that is quite other than the self; threatening, but at the same time attractive and of supreme value.

The 'holy' can only be described, however, in words that have a rational, everyday meaning – language which, if taken literally, does not do justice to the special quality of the experience. Many words seemed to describe the feelings and express ideas that were close to this experience of the 'holy' (goodness, wonder, purity, etc.) but none of them was actually about the holy itself. This set of words that attempt to describe the holy are (to use Otto's term) its 'schema'. The process of finding words by means of which to convey the implications of the holy is 'schematisation'. Religious language is just such a schema, whereas the 'holy' itself is an *a priori* category, and cannot be completely described in terms of the particular experiences by means of which it appears.

Examples:

1. You feel overwhelmed at the sight of a range of snow-capped mountains looming above you. Their sheer size and bulk, contrasting with your own minuscule body, gives you a 'tingle', a sense of wonder, a sense that somehow this changes the way you see yourself, that faced with this scene of absolute and almost terrifying beauty, your life cannot ever be quite the same again.

   You then try to describe the experience to a cynical friend. You cast around for suitable words. You cannot convey that 'tingle', unless, as a result of your description, he or she too can start to sense 'the holy'.

2. You watch a horror movie on television. You know that the parts are played by actors, that there is artificially constructed scenery. Yet, for all that, you feel the hairs bristle on the back of your neck, you may even feel a shudder, your heart may beat faster. Because of what you are seeing on the screen, and in spite of all the rational explanations, you are sensing something that is 'beyond' that immediate experience.

The holy, according to Otto, is something like each of those experiences. It cannot be fully explained, only experienced.

Otto's idea of schematisation is important for understanding the nature of the philosophy of religion. Philosophy examines the rational concepts by means of which the prime experience is schematised. The proofs of the existence of God are, following this way of thinking, not proofs of the actual existence of a being which is known and defined as 'God', but are rational ways of expressing the intuition about 'God' that comes as a result of religious experience.

Thus, the idea of the God as the designer of the universe is not open to logical proof (we have already seen the limitations of the 'designer' analogy) but is a schema, i.e. think what it would be like if this whole world had been designed for a particular purpose, with everything working together as it should; that (according to this schema) is something akin to what it means to believe in God. In fact, as we saw earlier, many examinations of the traditional proofs, by pointing out the logical limitations of such proof, but the validity of them as analogies or pointers to the idea of 'God', actually conform to what Otto describes (from his different starting point) as a schema.

Notice that this also applies to language. Taking the idea of models and qualifiers, there is the sense that the model is the result of the schema (God is like this or that) but that it is then qualified to show that it is not simply a literal description (e.g. the all-perfect ... or the absolute ...).

We see that the nature of religious language, the analysis of religious experience, and the logical examination of the traditional arguments, all point in the same direction – to an experience and a level of reality which transcends, but springs out of the literal, the empirical or the rational. All of these things can suggest the object of religious devotion, but none can define or describe it literally. This is why Paul Tillich insists on the symbolic nature of such religious language; it always points beyond itself.

IN OTHER WORDS:

In this chapter we have looked at the nature of religious language, the arguments for the existence of God and the nature of religious experience. The essential points are:

- the inadequacy of literal, empirically based language to express 'God';

- the limitations of logical argument to encompass religious intuition.

We have seen that religious language:

- is a 'schema' by which a person may seek to convey the inexpressible;

- is symbolic, not literal;

and that religious experience may involve:

- a sense of the unity of everything, and of oneself being at one with everything (mysticism).

- a sense of a presence of something quite extraordinary – terrifying, uncanny, fascinating, mysterious.

- a sense of the absolute rightness of something (Kant's categorical imperative).

- a general sense of the wonder of nature.

- a personal experience, resulting in a sense of value and commitment.

We now turn to two particular issues in the philosophy of religion: miracles and the problem of evil. Both involve rational arguments, but in neither does the rational do justice to the central religious questions.

—————————— Miracles ——————————

The cosmological arguments for the existence of God were an attempt to lead the mind from an understanding of the physical world to a reality that lay behind it and was responsible for it. The arguments led from ordinary movement and causes to the idea of an unmoved mover or uncaused cause. But the Western theistic religions have tended to go beyond this, and have seen the action of God in particular events, which may be called miracles. Initially we will be looking at miracles in terms of events for which there is no rational or scientific explanation. This is not the only type of miracle, and it raises some religious questions, but it will serve as a starting point.

If you want to find an argument against this idea of a miracle, the logical place to look is among those philosophers who take an empiricist position – for an empiricist will want to relate everything to the objects of sense experience, and this is precisely what is not possible if an event is to be a miracle in the particular sense that we are considering. A critique along these lines is given by Hume.

Hume examines the idea of miracles in the tenth book of his *Enquiry*

Concerning Human Understanding. His argument runs like this:

- A wise man proportions his belief to the evidence; the more evidence there is for something, the more likely it is to have been the case (see p. 25).
- Equally, the evidence of others is assessed according to their reliability as witnesses.

He then turns to the idea of miracles and offers a definition.

- A miracle is the violation of a law of nature.
- **But**, a law of nature is the result of a very large number of observations.

He therefore argues:

'A miracle is a violation of the laws of nature; and as a firm and unalterable experience has established these laws, the proof against a miracle, from the very nature of the fact, is as entire as any argument from experience can possibly be imagined. Why is it more probable that all men must die; that lead cannot, of itself, remain suspended in the air; that fire consumes wood, and is extinguished by water; unless it be, that these events are found agreeable to the laws of nature, and there is required a violation of these laws, or in other words, a miracle to prevent them? Nothing is esteemed a miracle if it ever happen in the common course of nature. ... The plain consequence is ... That no testimony is sufficient to establish a miracle, unless the testimony be of such a kind, that its falsehood would be more miraculous, than the fact, which it endeavours to establish.'

[from *Hume on Religion* ed. Wollheim, Fontana 1963 p.210f]

In other words, it is always more likely that the report of a miracle is mistaken, than that a law of nature was actually broken. For the evidence against the miracle will always be greater than the evidence for it.

For Hume, the only way in which, on balance, a miracle could be accepted, is if it would be a greater miracle if all the evidence for it were to be proved mistaken, than if a law of nature was broken. In practice, that rules out miracles, although strictly speaking it does not preclude a miracle, it simply says that there can never be sufficient evidence for a wise man to accept it as such.

Hume's argument is based on the assumption (which we accepted at the opening of this section) that a miracle is a violation of a law of nature, in other words, that the event is inexplicable in terms of scientific knowledge. But is that necessarily the case for an event to be a miracle?

Take the example of a 'black hole' in the middle of a galaxy. By what are generally called 'laws of nature' (according to Newtonian physics) a 'black hole' is a violation. It does not work as expected. Is it therefore seen as a miracle? Generally speaking, it is not. It is merely an extreme case, which suggests that physics needs to be modified to take it into account.

We therefore have to ask a further question: What distinguishes a miracle from a rare or unique occurrence?

Generally, in order to be termed a miracle, something needs to be seen as fitting into a scheme which displays positive purpose. If a life is saved, against all expectations, that may be regarded as a miracle by those for whom that life was dear. If a person suddenly drops dead, his or her friends will not see that as a positive contribution, and will therefore not call it a miracle. On the other hand, the long-lost relative, who had no emotional connection with the deceased, and who is suddenly saved from financial ruin by an unexpected legacy, may well find it miraculous.

In this way, the argument about miracles refers back to the argument from design. 'Is there an overall design and purpose to be seen in everything in general?' What the argument about miracles asks is 'Is there a design and purpose within some individual situations, as opposed to the generality of life?'

A unique occurrence (e.g. some previously unobserved event in a distant galaxy) is not called a miracle. It does not so much violate a law of nature as offer a spur to science to work out why it has occurred. It lacks the sense of personal relevance and purpose required for it to be a miracle.

If the event itself is not out of the ordinary – in other words, if there can be a perfectly reasonable explanation for it – it may still be regarded as a miracle if its timing is right. Thus the long-lost relative mentioned above might find that the legacy arrives at the same time as a final demand for payment of some impossibly large debt. Not that it has happened, but that it has happened **now**, is the remarkable thing.

rsal?

...rtant sense in which the idea of the miraculous and
...osmological and design arguments work against one
...he whole essence of the earlier arguments is that the world
...ured in a way that displays an overall purpose. Those arguments
only work on the basis of regularity, for only in regularity does the
sense of design and purpose appear. Yet the literal idea of a miracle
violates that regularity – introduces a sense of arbitrariness and
unpredictability into an understanding of the world which undermines
the cosmological structures.

IN OTHER WORDS:

- You can't have it both ways. **Either** God is seen to exist because
  the world is a wonderful, ordered place, **or** his hand is seen in
  individual events because the world is an unpredictable,
  miraculous place. It is not reasonable to try to argue for both at
  once, since the one appears to cancel out the other!

- An event is termed a miracle because it is thought to have a
  special value or purpose, not just because it is a rare occurrence.

The problem of evil

In its simplest form, the problem can be stated like this:

If God created the world
And if God is all-powerful and all-loving
Then Why is there is evil and suffering in the world?

Conclusion:

Either God is not all-powerful;
Or God is not all-loving;
Or Suffering is either unreal, necessary, or a means to a greater good;
Or The whole idea of an all-loving and all-powerful creator God was a
mistake in the first place.

An important book setting out the answers that have been suggested for this problem is *Evil and the God of Love* by John Hick. In it he gives two main lines of approach: the Augustinian and the Irenaean.

1. The Augustinian approach is named after St Augustine (354-430), and reflects his background in Neo-Platonism. In Plato's thought, particular things are imperfect copies of their 'forms'. Imperfection is a feature of the world as we experience it. The Augustinian approach to evil and suffering is to say that evil is not a separate force opposing the good, but is a lack of goodness, a deprivation. Human fallibility and human free will, on this argument, can lead to suffering and evil. The world as we experience it is full of imperfect copies, and suffering and evil are bound up with that imperfection. For Augustine, the Fall in the Garden of Eden meant that from then on humankind would be imperfect, and therefore liable to suffering and evil. But evil is not a positive force.

IN OTHER WORDS:

Hick (p.59f) uses the analogy of a half full or half empty glass: you can either choose to see your glass as half empty or half full. The Augustinian approach to the sadness of seeing that your glass is half empty, is to point out that it is in fact half full. Emptiness is not a thing in itself, but merely a lack of drink!

2. The Irenaean approach is named after Bishop Irenaeus of Lyons (c.130-c.202). It presents the idea that human life is imperfect, but having been made in the image of God, human beings are intended to grow and develop, aspiring to be what God intended them to be. Through free will and all the sufferings of life, people have an opportunity to grow and learn. Without a world in which there is both good and evil, that would be impossible:

How, if we had no knowledge of the contrary, could we have had instruction in that which is good? ... For just as the tongue receives experiences of sweet and bitter by means of tasting, and the eye discriminates between black and white by means of vision, and the ear recognises the distinctness of sounds by hearing; so also does the mind, receiving through the experience of both the knowledge of what is good, become the more tenacious in its preservation, by acting in obedience to God... But if any one do shun the knowledge of both kinds of things, and the twofold perception of knowledge,

he unaware divests himself of the character of a human being.
[*Against Heresies* quoted in Hick p.220; Fontana, 1968]

In other words, it is only by having a world in which there is both good and evil can we have moral choice and develop spiritually.

Hick's own approach to the problem of evil is one that treats evil as something to be tackled and overcome, but with the hope that, ultimately, it will be seen as part of an overall divine plan.

Some general remarks

There are, of course, many religious issues that could be examined here, but from the standpoint of philosophy notice how the problem of evil relates back to the traditional arguments for the existence of God, and indeed to the metaphysical systems that lie behind them:

- Is the world fundamentally an imperfect copy of something more real? As we look at the world, do we see it as a half empty glass? Both the ontological and cosmological arguments look beyond the partial experience of 'greatness' or movement or causality, to something than which none greater can be conceived, an unmoved mover, or an uncaused cause. The mind is led from a present experience of a half empty glass to the conception of what a full glass would be like – a perfection which underpins this imperfect world.

- Or is the world still developing, working towards a perfection that lies in the future? Is the structure of the world (along with everything in it, good and bad) the means by which growth can take place? The argument from design and the moral argument have a contribution to make to this point of view. Darwin's evolution through natural selection is based on the facts of suffering and death which allow only the strongest members of a species to survive and breed. Without suffering and death, no evolution! In Marxist theory the class struggle, with all the suffering that it involves, is the means of bringing about a classless society in the future.

These are practical, moral and political as well as religious questions. But they raise an enormous philosophical question:

Everything that we experience is in a process of change. Birth, death, suffering and evil are all part of that process. (Even if, following Augustine, you say that evil is a deprivation of good, rather than a positive force in itself, you still have to admit that deprivation of good is part of that process.)

Where do you find reality?

- Is reality to be found in an ideal realm outside, over and above the flux of life? [Line up behind Plato, Augustine, Aquinas and most traditional theists!]

- Is reality to be found as an end product to be arrived at through this process of change? [Line up behind Irenaeus, Darwin, Marx and evolutionary thinkers like Teilhard de Chardin!]

- Is reality to be found within life itself, including all its limitations and changes? [Line up behind Heraclitus, Spinoza and the Buddha!]

For reflection:

An important contribution to philosophy as a whole made by the philosophy of religion is the way it highlights the inadequacy of literal language to encompass the whole of life. Although much of it has been concerned with the idea of 'God', the sort of discussion presented in this chapter could be used equally with issues of aesthetics (what we mean by beauty or by art) or morality. Mystical experience and a religious sense of awe are reflected in many common human experiences: falling in love, looking at a beautiful scene, being moved by music. An essential quality of all such experiences is that they require a great flexibility of language if they are to be described – there is always an elusive 'something more' about them.

3

MIND AND BODY

'It was on a dreary night of November, that I beheld the accomplishment of my toils. With an anxiety that almost amounted to agony, I collected the instruments of life around me, that I might infuse a spark of being into the lifeless thing that lay at my feet. It was already one in the morning; the rain pattered dismally against the panes, and my candle was nearly burnt out, when by the glimmer of the half-extinguished light, I saw the dull yellow eye of the creature open; it breathed hard, and a convulsive motion agitated its limbs.'

[*Frankenstein*, 1818]

Thus Mary Shelley describes the moment of triumph and disaster for Victor Frankenstein in her novel. He had sought the origin of life by a process of analysis, dissecting the human body and exploring its various components. He had observed the changes that take place on death, the corruption of the various organs, and had longed to reverse that process, to bring life back to the dead. Then he collected the 'materials' for his experiment – all the various bits of human anatomy – and fashioned them into a human-like creature. Eventually he finds the secret of their animation, and in that horrifying moment, the creature which he has fitted together comes to life. (In Shelley's novel details of this process are not given, but later film treatments of the Frankenstein story have generally focused on electricity – the 'spark of life' being brought about by the sparks of electrical discharge.)

Released into the world, the 'creature', not fully human and shunned by society, nevertheless develops human emotions, reasoning and skills. Filled with both tenderness and rage, longing for a mate of his own kind and murderously angry with Frankenstein for creating him thus, he asks 'Who am I?'

The 'philosophy of mind', or 'philosophical psychology', is that branch of philosophy which undertakes the Frankenstein-like task on analysing bodies, minds and persons, dissecting them and attempting to re-animate them, in order to understand the nature of intelligent life.

As you read this book, your eyes are scanning from left to right, your fingers turn the pages, your brain is consuming energy, taking oxygen from its blood supply, tiny electrical impulses are passing between brain cells. All that is part of the physical world, and can be detected scientifically. How does all that relate to the process of reading, thinking, learning and remembering? And how do both relate to personal identity?

If, as the result of an accident, I were to have an arm or leg amputated, I should refer to the detached member as 'my arm' or 'my leg', not in the sense that I owned it, but that I regarded it as part of myself, a part which I must now do without. In the same way, I can list all the parts of myself: my hair, my face, my body, my mind, my emotions, my attitudes. Some of these will be parts of my mental make-up, others will be parts of my physical body.

Where in all this is the real 'me'?

- Am I to be identified with my physical body? With my mind?
- Am I somehow a collection of all these things?
- Do I exist outside my body?
- If so, could I continue to exist after the death of my body?
- Is my mind the same thing as my brain?
- If not, then where is my mind?
- Can I ever really know other people's minds, or do I just look, listen and guess what they're thinking?
- What about computer-created artificial intelligence?

These are just some of the questions that are explored within the philosophy of mind. Its issues relate to biology, psychology, sociology, computer science, and all possible matters related to human thought, memory, communication and personal identity. But we shall start with a basic question, which opens up many of these issues: How is my mind related to my body?

The relationship between mind and body

Philosophy has explored a whole range of possible relationships between mind and body. At one extreme there is the idea that only the physical body and its activity is real (**materialism** and **behaviourism**), at the other is the rarer idea that everything is fundamentally mental (**idealism**). Most philosophers come to a view that both bodies and minds have distinct but related realities (**dualism**). How exactly they are related is a further problem, and so our consideration of dualism has many sub-theories.

Materialism

A materialist attempts to explain everything in terms of physical objects, and tends to deny the reality of anything that cannot be reduced to them. So, for a materialist, the mind or 'self' is nothing more than a way of describing physical bodies and their actions, including brain activity. We may experience something as a thought or emotion, but in fact it is nothing more than electrical impulses in the brain, or chemical or other reactions in the rest of the body. Points to consider:

- Apply electrical shocks to the brain, and the personality can be affected. (This is the basis of a form of treatment for severe depression, simulating epileptic fits.)
- A person who suffers brain damage is no longer the same, the character is changed. In severe cases he or she may not appear to be a person at all, but merely a living body, devoid of all the normal attributes of mind.

Do these examples confirm the materialist view?

Materialism takes a reductionist approach to mental activit. A reductionist view is one that suggests, for example, that:

- Music is nothing but a set of vibrations in the air.
- A painting is nothing but coloured dots of paint on canvas.
- **So** a person is nothing but a brain, attached to a body and nervous system.

The 'nothing but' distinguishes materialism from other theories, for nobody would deny that, in some sense, a person is related to a brain, in the same way as a symphony is related to air movements. The essential question is whether or not it is possible to express what a 'something more' might be, if the materialist position seems inadequate.

For reflection:

You see people waving to you and smiling.

- Does that indicate that they are friendly? That they have minds as well as bodies? That they have freely chosen to act in that way?

- Let us analyse what is actually happening:
  – you see an arm moving;
  – within that arm, muscles are contracting;
  – the contraction is caused by chemical changes, brought about by electrical impulses from the brain;
  – those impulses are caused by electrical activity in the brain;
  – that activity depends on consuming energy and having an adequate oxygen supply via the blood;
  – nutrition and oxygen are taken in from the environment;
  – and so on, and so on.

- The act of waving is explained in terms of a material chain of cause and effect. That chain is, for practical purposes, infinite – it depends upon the whole way in which the universe is constructed. There is no point in that chain for some 'mind' to have its say – the world of sense experience is a closed system, and everything in it is totally determined. That is a materialist perspective, but (as far as the idea of a closed system of causes is concerned) it also follows from the ideas of Kant, for whom the phenomena of experience were determined, and causality was imposed on them by the human mind. The difference between the materialist and Kant is that Kant holds that there are minds and things-in-themselves but we cannot know them through sense experience, whereas the materialist accepts nothing other than the material world known to the senses.

'Behaviourism' is the term used for the rather crude materialist theory that mental phenomena are in fact simply physical phenomena. Crying out and rubbing a part of the body is what pain is about. Shouting and waving a fist is what anger is about. All mental states are reduced by the behaviourist to things that can be observed and measured. People usually take a behaviourist position because they hold a radical empirical view of philosophy – everything must be reduced to sensations.

The problem is that we experience a difference between a sensation or thought and the physical movement or the words that result from it. I can think before I speak, or before I write, but for a behaviourist there is nothing other than the words or the writing. To know a feeling, for a behaviourist, one must observe behaviour.

Idealism

The opposite of materialism is idealism: that reality is mental rather than physical. What we see of our body, and the bodies of others, are sense experiences; and these, after all, are simply impressions we get in our minds. We saw in the first chapter that Descartes, realising that his senses could always be deceived, came to the view that 'I think, therefore I am' as the starting point for philosophy. All he knew for certain was the fact of his own thought. Descartes used that fact as a basis for a dualist viewpoint, for he did not deny the reality of bodies, whereas a strict idealist holds that mind is the only reality.

A criticism of the idealist approach might be that, although we may not be certain of the existence of matter, for all practical purposes we have to assume it. However much other people are merely sense impressions in our mind, we infer that there are people with minds and bodies like ours that are causing those impressions. Two idealist philosophers were mentioned in chapter one: Berkeley (see p22) and Leibniz (see p32).

Dualism

If neither the materialist nor the idealist position convinces you by its account for the relationship between mind and body, the answer may be sought in some form of dualism: that mind and body are distinct and very different things. Each is seen as part of the self, part of what it means to be a person, but the question then becomes: How do these two things interact?

This question has a long history. Plato, in *Phaedo*, argued for the immortality of the soul on two grounds:

1. That the body was composite, and was therefore perishable, whereas the mind was simple, and therefore imperishable.
2. That the mind had knowledge of the universals, the eternal forms (such as 'goodness itself') rather than individual events and objects. Because it relates to the immortal realm (the forms being immortal, because not particular), the soul is itself immortal and able to survive the body.

Few people today would wish to take up these arguments in the form that Plato presented them. But they persist in two widely accepted features of the mind/body question:

1. That the mind is not within space/time and not material – and thus that it should not be identified with its material base in the brain.
2. That the mind functions through communication – is not simply limited to the operations of a single particular body, i.e. the mind is not subject to physical limitations, and is related to transpersonal communication.

Descartes' starting point in the quest for knowledge, 'I think, therefore I am', implied a radical distinction between the world of matter, known to the senses, and the mental world, known (at least in one's own case) directly. They are two different realms, distinct but interacting. The mind, for Descartes, is able to deflect the flow of physical currents in the nervous system, and thus influence the mechanical working of the physical body. For Descartes, there has to be a point of interaction, for in all other respects he considers the material world to be controlled by mechanical forces, and without a mental component to make a difference, there would be no way in which a mental decision to do something could influence that mechanical world.

One danger here is to imagine the mind as some kind of subtle, invisible body, existing in the world of space and time, yet not subject to its usual rules of cause and effect. This, of course, is a rather crude caricature of what Descartes and other dualists have actually claimed. (It is also an important caricature, having been used by Ryle in *The Concept of Mind* (1949), a most influential book for an understanding of the mind/body issue, where he called the Cartesian view the 'official view' and labelled the mind 'the ghost in the machine'.)

The essential thing for Descartes is that mental reality is not empirical and therefore not in the world of space. The mind is not located in the body – it may be related to the body, but is not some occult alternative set of physical causes and effects. It is therefore a matter of debate whether Ryle was justified in calling Descartes' view 'the ghost in the machine', although a popular form of dualism may well give that impression.

Various forms of dualism

Epiphenomenalism This view is that the brain and nervous system are so complex that they give the impression of individuality and free choice. Although totally controlled by physical laws, we therefore 'seem' to have an independent mind. This is the closest that a dualistic view comes to materialism. The essential thing here is that mind does not influence the body – mind is just the product of the complexity of the body's systems.

The various things that I think, imagine, picture in my mind are epiphenomena. They arise out of and are caused by the electrical impulses that move between brain cells, but they are not actually part of that phenomenon – they are 'above' (epi-) those phenomena.

> Imagine a robot, programmed by computer. A simple version could be the source of amusement, as it attempts to mimic human behaviour. But as the memory capacity of the computer in increased, the process of decision making in the programme is so complex that the computer takes on a definite character. In this case, the character can be seen to be a product of the computer's memory – that would be epiphenomenalism. (We shall examine artificial intelligence later in this chapter.)

Interactionism Most forms of dualism claim that the mind and the body are distinct but act upon one another. For example, if you have tooth decay (a bodily phenomenon) it will lead to pain (a mental experience); the body is affecting the mind. Equally, if you are suddenly afraid, you can break out in a cold sweat and start to shake; the mind is affecting the body. Although they interact, the mind and body remain distinct and appear self contained. Thus (to take up the example of the person waving), an interactionist would not say that there is some break within the series of causes that led to the arm waving. The physical world remains a closed system within the body, but the whole of that system is influenced by the mind, and responds to its wishes. But how exactly is this interaction to come about? Here are some theories:

Occasionalism:

On the occasion of my being hit over the head with a cricket bat, there is a simultaneous but uncaused feeling of pain! The two systems (physical and mental) do not have a direct causal connection. The philosopher Malebranche suggested that whenever he wanted to move his arm, it was actually moved by God.

Pre-established harmony:

The physical and mental realms are separate and independent processes. Each appears to influence the other, but in fact they are independent but running in harmony. This view was put forward by Geulinx, a Dutch follower of Descartes. It is also found in Leibniz, who holds that ultimately everything is divisible again and again until you arrive at monads – simple entities without extension, and therefore mental. These monads cannot act upon one another, for each develops according to its own nature. But a complex being comprises countless monads. How do they all work together to produce intelligent activity? Leibniz argued that there must be a pre-established harmony, organising the otherwise independent monads. As far as human persons are concerned, Leibniz holds that there is a dominant monad (a soul) and that God has established that the other monads that form the complex person work in harmony with it.

Note:

'Pre-established harmony' may seem one of the most bizarre of the mind-body theories, but in Leibniz it has a very specific purpose, and one which has important implications for both metaphysics and the philosophy of religion. Leibniz was concerned to preserve the idea of 'teleology' (i.e. that the world is organised in a purposeful way) in the face of the mechanistic science and philosophy of his day.

If everything is locked into a series of causes, what room is left for a sense of purpose or for God? Leibniz' answer is that the individual monads of which everything is comprised do not actually effect one another. Rather, God has established a harmony by which they can work together.

Double aspect theory   This is the view, sometimes called the 'identity hypothesis', that ideas and the operations of bits of the brain are simply two aspects of the same thing. Thinking is thus the inner aspect of which the outer aspect is brain activity. (Perhaps we could say that music is the inner cultural aspect of which sound waves of particular frequencies are the outer physical aspect.)

Of course, if the identity hypothesis is correct, there is a problem with freedom. Brain activity, like all physical processes, is limited by physical laws and is in theory predictable. But if mental events are simply another aspect of these physical events, they must also be limited by physical laws. If all my action is theoretically predictable, how can I be free?

Spinoza argued that everything is both conscious and extended; all reality has both a mental and a physical aspect. The mind and body cannot be separated, and therefore there can be no life beyond this physical existence. Spinoza also held that freedom was an illusion, caused by the fact that we simply do not know all the real causes of our decisions.

IN OTHER WORDS:

Either everything is material and mind is an illusion;

Or everything is mintal, and the material body is an illusion;

Or there are both minds and bodies, distinct by reacting on one another.

- Of course, you may feel that there is something fundamentally wrong with looking at bodies and minds in this way. If so, perhaps Ryle's approach may be more in line with your thinking ...

——— The Concept of Mind ———

In *The Concept of Mind* (1949) Gilbert Ryle suggests that to speak of minds and bodies as though they were equivalent things is a 'category mistake'. To explain what he means by this he used the example of someone visiting a university and seeing many different colleges, libraries and research laboratories. The visitor then asks 'But where is the University?' The answer, of course, is that there is no university over and above all its component parts that have already been visited. The term university is a way of describing all of these things together

– it is a term from another category, not the same category as the individual components.

In the same way, Ryle argued that you should not expect to find a 'mind' over and above all the various parts of the body and its actions, for 'mind' is a term from another category, a way of describing bodies and the way in which they operate. This he claims is the fundamental flaw in the traditional dualistic approach to mind and body (which he attributes to Descartes and terms the 'ghost in the machine'):

> 'When two terms belong to the same category, it is proper to construct conjunctive propositions embodying them. Thus a purchaser may say that he bought a left-hand glove and a right-hand glove, but not that he bought a left-hand glove, a right-hand glove and a pair of gloves.... Now the dogma of the Ghost in the Machine does just this. It maintains that there exist both bodies and minds; that there occur physical processes and mental processes; that there are mechanical causes of corporeal movements and mental causes of corporeal movements. I shall argue that these and other analogous conjunctions are absurd; but, it must be noticed, the argument will not show that either of the illegitimately conjoined propositions is absurd in itself. I am not, for example, denying that there occur mental processes. Doing long division is a mental process and so is making a joke. But I am saying that the phrase 'there occur mental processes' does not mean the same sort of thing as 'there occur physical processes', and, therefore, that it makes no sense to conjoin or disjoin the two.'
>
> [Ryle, *The Concept of Mind*, Peregrine Books p.23]

For Ryle, talking about minds is a particular way of talking about bodies and their activity. Remember, however, that Ryle is primarily concerned with language – his book is about what we mean when we speak about the 'mind'. What he shows is that, in ordinary language, 'mind' terms actually describe activities performed by the body, or are at least based on such activities. We speak about the mind of another person without claiming to have any privileged information about their inner mental operations.

An example:

If I say that someone is intelligent, I do so on the basis of what he or she has said or done. Descriptions of mental states depend

---

upon information provided by physical bodies, activities and forms of communication.

- Think of a person you know.
- Consider exactly what it is you mean when you describe that person's personality or mind. Think of particular qualities that you would ascribe to him or her.
- Consider the evidence you could give to back up your view of these qualities.
- Consider what would have to happen in order for you to be persuaded that you were mistaken about him or her.

Clearly, we can get to know another person, but, if Ryle is correct and there is no 'inner' self to be found, in what therefore does the personality consist? His answer is in terms of 'dispositions'. These are the qualities that make me what I am; the propensity to behave in a particular way in a particular situation.

If I say that someone is 'irritable' I do not mean that I have some privileged access to an 'irritability factor' in their mind, I just mean that, given a situation that is not to his or her liking, he or she is likely to start complaining, sulking, etc. In other words, the irritability is simply a way of describing a disposition.

Thus, for Ryle, the ascription of mental predicates (clever, etc.) does not require the existence of a separate, invisible thing called a mind. The description 'clever' indeed refers to the way in which something is done, but, equally, cleverness cannot be defined simply in terms of that action. What is clever for one person might not be so for another, and the mental description refers to the way in which the individual person habitually relates to the world, and the expectation a person would have of him or her, rather than some special quality of an action that makes it clever.

An example:

A child is 'clever' if it learns to stagger to its feet and totter a few paces forward before collapsing down on the ground again. The same is not claimed for the drunk who performs a similar set of movements. If Ryle wishes to dismiss the 'ghost in the machine' he must equally dismiss the 'ghost in the action', for mental predicates refer to, but are not defined by, individual actions.

One particular difficulty with identifying a mental phenomena with physical actions is illustrated by the idea of pain.

- I may shout, cry, hold the afflicted part of my body, I may scream and roll on the ground, curl up, look ashen. But none of these things is actually the same thing as the pain I am experiencing. The pain is indicated by them, but not defined by them.
- I may watch an actor performing all the things listed above. But because he or she is acting, I do not imagine that there is any actual pain.
- Yet, if being in pain is actually identified with those things (as Ryle implies), then the actor is in pain.

COMMENT:

Much modern debate on the mind/body issue has been prompted by Ryle's critique of dualism. One feature of his work that one should keep in mind is that his approach is linguistic. He asks what it means to ascribe mental predicates. The question remains of this or any similar approach, whether the meaning of the mental predicate is the same as its method of verification. I can verify my description of someone as clever by observing and listening to him or her. But is the information I receive in that way identical with what I mean by cleverness? Or is cleverness hinted at by, but not defined by such information?

—————— A 'place' for mind? ——————

A basic question for mind/body, as for many other areas of philosophy, Does something exist if it does not have a place within the world of space and time?

It is clear, for example, following Ryle, that there is no place for a 'self' or 'soul' alongside the body. Everything to which language about the mind refers has its own place in the world – the clever action, the kindly word – and he is right in saying that the criterion for saying that these words 'clever' and 'kindly' refer, not so some occult substance, but to the way in which particular deeds are performed.

But the dualist is not actually saying that the mind exists physically outside the body – the dualist position is that the mind is not extended, that is does not exist within time and space. We have returned, therefore, to the fundamental philosophical issue of reductionism. Consider any piece of music:

- It comprises a sequence of sound waves within the air.
- There is no music apart from those sound waves. For even if I have a tune running in my head (a problematic thing for any philosopher to say), what I am doing is recalling that pattern of sound waves.
- All the qualities of music (its ability to move one emotionally, its sense of beauty, of completeness, its ability to calm) have as their source that series of sound waves.
- The language a musician uses to describe a piece of music is quite different from the language a physicist uses to describe sound waves.
- There is no hidden, secret music that exists alongside the sound waves – rather, the sound waves are the physical medium through which music is generated.
- **Therefore** it really should not be too difficult to see that the brain, along with the nervous system and all the physical activities (including speech) that it controls, is the physical medium through which a mind expresses itself.

There have been many forms of the problem of how the body and mind are related, but most can be seen, in one way or another, to be a result of an attempt to express the interconnectedness and yet distinctness of physical and non-physical reality.

What is clear from recent neurophysics, is that the brain is extremely complex, that it controls not just the autonomic nervous system, but also those elements that we describe as personality or mind.

It is equally clear that an essential feature of mind is communication. It is difficult to see how one could describe a mind that did not communicate – and in communicating, by words, facial expressions, writing, the qualities of that mind are shared. It is no more sensible to try to analyse an isolated human brain in the hope of discovering the seeds of cultural history, than it is taking a Stradivarius apart, in order to discover why a violin concerto can be so moving!

———— Neurones and computers ————

In *The Astonishing Hypothesis: The Scientific Search for the Soul* (Simon & Schuster, 1994) Francis Crick asks how it is that, if the brain is a machine made up of nerve cells and neurones, it can also take on the functions of what we know as mind; appreciating colour, telling jokes, thinking through problems. He argues that the brain has 'awareness neurones', which are the physical basis of mind. He believes that the 'soul' is physically located in the head, and that research into brain activity will come to reveal the processes which we call consciousness.

In suggesting this, he rejects two common conceptions. The first (from a dualistic standpoint) is that the soul or mind is not physically located in the body, but is external, and may be able to survive the death of the body. The second is the 'homunculus' idea: that the soul is distinct from the brain, but located inside the head, like a person within a person. This, Crick believes, solves nothing.

He argues that a complex structure has characteristics that go beyond those of its component parts. (So, for example, a city has a character over and above those of its individual citizens.) Therefore the 'soul', or mind, is the product of the interactions of the billions of brain cells. The human brain is, after all, the most complex thing known in the universe. He suggests that only a part of the brain is involved with consciousness. Most of it controls the various functions that keep us alive.

He accepts that we are probably still some way off from an understanding of these 'awareness neurones', but his essential point is that the more science comes to understand the operations of various parts of the brain, the more it will be apparent that all of what we know as 'mind' will be found within it.

Notice what Crick's work can and cannot claim. If these 'awareness neurones' are identified, they may be recognised as the physical basis of mind, in exactly the same way that DNA is the physical and chemical basis of life. (Crick was awarded a Nobel Prize in 1962 for his part in the discovery of DNA.) Now, since the discovery of DNA, it is accepted that the characteristics of the physical body are given in its unique DNA molecule, hence the possibility of DNA fingerprinting. But that does not mean that the physical body is 'nothing but' a DNA code, simply that it is as it is because of it. In the same way, the 'awareness neurones' may one day be shown to be the basis of mind and personality. But that does not mean that the mind is 'reduced' to them.

IN OTHER WORDS:

- Our DNA does not show where we live, or what experiences we have. It makes us unique, it enables all the cells in our body to grow and work together, but it does not make us a 'person'. It can identify us from traces of body tissue, but it cannot describe us as living beings. Life is based on DNA; but life is not the same thing as DNA.

- The discovery of 'consciousness neurones' would not actually explain why people have the thoughts they have – it would only show the physical basis that enables them to have thoughts in the first place.

- Your 'consciousness neurones' will not be 'you' any more than your DNA is 'you'.

AI and neural computing

To appreciate how the brain might be thought to create the mind, one can look at two different areas of computer science:

- Artificial intelligence (AI) uses computers to perform some of the functions of the human brain. It works on the basis of knowledge and response, the computer stores memories and is programmed to respond to present situations which correspond to them. It can, for example, recognise words, and can respond to them. The bigger the computer memory, the more 'life-like' does this form of artificial intelligence become.

- Neural computing goes about its task quite differently. Although, like AI, it is based on a computer, it tries to produce a computer which actually works like a human brain – recognising things, forming mental images, even dreaming and feeling emotions. A neural computer, although very simple by comparison, actually works like a human brain.

Some scientists claim that AI holds the key. The human brain, they argue, comprises about 100 million memories and a few thousand functions. All you need, in a sense, is raw computing power. On the other hand, this is never going to be that easy, because the human brain, being the most complex thing known in the universe, will take a great deal of computer power to match it. This view is countered by those who claim that neural computing holds the key to an understanding of the 'mind', since a neural computer can take on characteristics that are normally regarded as 'human'. Human brains are not programmed, they just learn, and that is the difference with a neural computer – it does not have to be fed all its information, it learns it itself.

IN OTHER WORDS:

AI is the attempt to store and reproduce the workings of already developed brains (of those who programme the computers); neural computing is the attempt to get a simple brain to 'grow' in intelligence.

This debate between AI and neural computing highlights a feature of Ryle's argument in *The Concept of Mind*. Ryle made the distinction between 'knowing that' and 'knowing how'. He argues that to do something intelligently is not just a matter of knowing facts, but of applying them – to use information and not just to store it. To do something skilfully implies an operation over and above applying already established rules. To give one of Ryle's examples – a clock keeps time, and it set to do so, but it is not seen as intelligent. He speaks of the 'intellectualist legend' which is that a person who acts intelligently first has to think of the various rules that apply to his or her action, and then think how to apply them (thus making 'knowing how' just part of 'knowing that'), knowing the rules for action as well as the facts upon which that action is based.

Ryle claims that when, for example, we make a joke, we do not actually know the rules by which something is said to be funny. We do not perform two actions – first thinking of the rules, and then trying to apply them. Rather, we simply say something that, in spite of not knowing why, actually strikes us as funny.

The same could be said for a work of art, literature or musical composition. The second-rate composer follows all the established rules and applies them diligently. He or she produces art that follows fashion. The really creative person does not follow rules, producing work that may be loathed or controversial, but nevertheless may be said to be an intelligent production – the attempt to express something which goes beyond all previous experience or rules. This is a kind of 'knowing how': knowing how to perform creatively.

Now, if a computer is fed with sufficient information, it 'knows that'. It can also follow the process that Ryle calls the 'intellectualist legend' – it can sort out the rules first and then apply them to its new data. What it cannot do – unless we claim that it suddenly 'takes on a life of its own' – is to go beyond all the established (programmed) rules and do something utterly original.

By contrast with AI, neural networks offer the possibility that this might one day be the case. A neural network responds to each new experience by referring back to its memory of past experiences. In this way, it learns in the immediate context of its experience, not by pre-determined rules. It is more like a human being. Everything is judged (by the neural network as well as by the human being) in terms of past experiences and responses – and so its understanding of the world is constantly changing, being modified with each new experience. Its understanding is based on the relationships between events, not on rules.

Some philosophers, while accepting that the brain is the origin of consciousness, are suspicious of the computer-view of consciousness. John Searle, of the University of California, Berkeley, believes that consciousness is part of the physical world, even though it is experienced as private and subjective. He suggests that the brain causes consciousness in the same sense that the stomach causes digestion. The mind does not stand outside the ordinary physical processes of the world. On the other hand, he does not accept that this issue will be solved by computer programmes, and has called the computer-view of consciousness a 'pre-scientific superstition'.

There is something of a battlefield, therefore, between neuroscientists and neurophilosophers. All seem to hold that the mind is in some way the product of brain activity, but it is not at all clear what consciousness is. Some hold that it is a higher order mental activity (thinking about thinking: being self-conscious), others claim that it is the sensations that the body receives being recognised and related to one another by the brain.

So, for example, Professor Roger Penrose of Oxford (in *The Emperor's New Mind*, 1989) argued that it would be impossible to create an intelligent robot because consciousness requires self-awareness – and that is something that a computer cannot simulate. He argues that consciousness is based on a 'non-algorithmic' ingredient (in other words, an ingredient which does not depend on an algorithm; a set of rules). Yet, although this applies to AI, it does not necessarily apply to neural networks – for neural computing gets away from the idea that intelligence requires pre-programming with rules.

For consideration:

A robot would not need self-awareness in order to carry out actions intelligently – merely a set of goals to be achieved. So, for example, a chess programme can play chess and beat its own creator – it only knows what constitutes winning at chess, not what it means to play a game.

Perhaps one feature of the mind/body debate that has been highlighted in recent years by artificial intelligence and neural networking is that it is no longer adequate to accept a simple 'ghost in the machine' view of bodies and minds. Ryle's attack on this was based on language – reflecting the fact that people did not speak as though a body had a separate 'ghost' controlling it. What we now find is that, as the mechanistic view of the universe gives way to something rather more sophisticated, the nature of 'intelligent' activity is probably a feature of complexity and of relationships. In other words, if something is complex enough, and if its operation is based on a constantly changing pattern of relationships between its memory components, then it appears to evolve in a personal and intelligent way; it takes on character.

Chinese writing

A most graphic way of exploring the difference between being able to handle and manipulate information (which a computer can do very efficiently) and actually understanding that information (which, it is claimed a computer cannot), was given by the philosopher John Searle (in his Reith Lectures, 1984, *Minds, Brains and Science.*):

You are locked in a room, into which are passed various bits of Chinese writing – none of which you can read. You are then given instructions (in English) about how to relate one piece of Chinese to another – the result is that you are apparently able to respond in Chinese to instructions given in Chinese – but

---

without actually understanding one word of it. Searle argues that this is the case with computers – they can sort out bits of information, based on the instructions that they are given, but they cannot actually understand the information they are given.

The philosopher Hubert Dreyfus has given a criticism of AI based on an aspect of the philosophy of Heidegger. Heidegger (and Dreyfus) argued that human activity is a matter of skilfully coping with situations, and this presupposes a 'background', which is all the facts about society and life in general which lead us to do what we do. Now AI, according to Dreyfus, attempts to reduce this 'background' to a set of facts ('know-how' is reduced to 'know-that'). But this is an impossible task, because there can be an ever-growing number of facts to be taken into account – for practical purposes the number of background facts is infinite. Also, a person has to select which of those facts are relevant to the decision in hand – and the rules for deciding which are going to be relevant form another practically infinite sets of facts. This failure ever to provide enough rules and facts to give the background for a human decision is, according to Dreyfus (see Dreyfus H & Dreyfus S Mind over Machines, NY 1986), a problem which will continue to be formidable for AI.

For reflection:

It seems to me that Artificial Intelligence is basically a modern computerised form of Frankenstein's experiment! It is assembling 'materials' (in this case raw computer power and the data upon which it is to work) in the hope that is will find the key to make this become a thinking being, a self. So far, the AI limbs have started to twitch, but the monster has not taken on human form!

BACKGROUND NOTES:

A person's view on the mind/body issue depends on his or her general view of the world and our knowledge of it. It is possible to trace the debate through the history of philosophy. For example:
- Plato sees the soul as eternal, trapped in a limited material body.
- Aristotle sees the soul as the 'form' of the body (everything for him has both substance and form) – giving it unity.

- For Descartes ('I think therefore I am') the mind is primary.
- Hume said (in his Treatise on Human Nature)
  '...when I enter most intimately into what I call *myself,* I always stumble on some particular perception or other, of heat or cold, light or shade, love or hatred, pain or pleasure. I never can catch *myself* at any time without a perception, and never can observe any thing but the perception.'

(Hume, the empiricist, analysing the phenomenon of life, finds just the same thing when he analyses himself. He always sees some particular thing. For Hume, the world is an assembly of bits and pieces, regulated by general laws of nature – similarly, the self is an assembly of bits and pieces. He cannot see a general 'self' because he cannot step outside the world of phenomena.)

- Kant – I am phenomenally conditioned but noumenally free, therefore the mind is beyond the categories that apply to sense experience.

There is also a tradition which puts the mind quite beyond what can be known. So, for example, Wittgenstein, at the end of the *Tractatus,* says: 'The subject does not belong to the world, but it is a limit of the world.' In other words, from the standpoint of empirical evidence, I do not exist. As I experience it, the world is everything that is not me – although it includes my own physical body.

Personal identity

We now turn to some implications of the mind/body problem, particularly those that affect individuals in terms of their self-understanding, identity and knowledge of other people.

Free will

Freedom of the will is a major feature in the mind/body debate. If, as a materialist or even a epiphenomenalist would claim, the 'mind' is simply a by-product of brain activity, and if that brain activity, being part of a material world, is in theory totally predictable, then there is no such thing as free will. We appear to be free only because we do not understand the unique combination of causes which force us to make our particular decisions. We are pawns of fate – if all causes were known, we would have no freedom and no responsibility for what we (erroneously) call our 'mental' operations.

Clearly, if freedom and morality are seen as part of what it means to be a human individual – and are regarded as part of the human phenomenon – then it is impossible to see the mind as 'nothing more than' a by-product of brain activity.

Disembodied consciousness

This issue covers two areas – life after death and 'out of body' experiences. There is difficulty is getting firm evidence for these things, partly because, from a materialistic standpoint, they cannot happen, and therefore the person reporting them may be assumed to be mistaken. On the other hand, convictions about them will affect the view a person takes on the mind/body issue, since they imply a dualistic view.

From the religious point of view, life after death is linked to:

1. A sense of appropriate compensation, good or bad, for what a person has done during his or her life. All religious traditions have some element of reward or punishment – whether externally imposed (as in Western religions) or self generated (as the 'karma' of Eastern traditions).

2. The sense that human life somehow goes beyond the confines of a fragile human body – 'This cannot be everything: there must be something more.'

Neither of these constitutes evidence for survival of death. What they do show is the appropriateness of such belief for a religious person, and the reasons why he or she might hold to it in the absence of evidence.

Quite apart from religious considerations there are claims about the direct experience of something which is believed to be connected with the dead – ghosts, and communication with the dead. Again, although there is a great amount of evidence for strange phenomena in this field, such evidence is always open to interpretation, and a person who takes a strictly materialist standpoint will always find an alternative explanation.

'Out of body' experiences are generally associated with times of personal crisis or physical danger – e.g. while having an operation.

Some people have the sense that they have left their physical body 'down there' and are able to move away from it, observing it as from a distance.

About one in three people who come near to death in this way report a 'near-death experience' – so it is not a rare phenomenon, and it is not limited to people of any particular set of religious or other beliefs.

An example:

I was in a great deal of discomfort and pain. Suddenly, the sounds of the ward – the nurses bustling about, women laughing, the babies crying – all disappeared, and I just floated gently away from my bed – sideways at first, then up.

I know it sounds extraordinary, but I knew that I was dying. It was extraordinary, because all the pain and discomfort disappeared and I was conscious of light surrounding me, and I was warm – it was a beautiful feeling.

But then I thought of my mother, with whom I have a very strong bond, and I remember thinking that I can't do this to my Mum. I made a conscious effort to return to my body, which I did – with a great jolt, as if I'd been thrown back. And immediately all the pain returned.

(*Sunday Telegraph* 30 January 1994, p.11)

These experiences are being investigated to see if they can represent a genuine spacial removal from the physical body, or if they are simply the result of the imagination. If they proved to be literally true, they suggest that the mind/body relationship is dualistic, and that – even if related closely to the brain – the mind is not physically limited to the brain.

In all cases of unusual experiences, one test that can be applied is that which Hume applied to the accounts of miracles (see above p 68) – which is more likely, that the event actually happened as reported, or that the person reporting it is mistaken?

Knowledge of other minds

In a strictly dualistic view of bodies and minds, you cannot have direct knowledge of the minds of others. You can know their words, their actions, their writings, their facial and other body signals – but you cannot get access to their minds. For a dualist, knowledge of other minds therefore comes by analogy. I know what it is like to be me – I know that, when I speak, I am expressing something that I am thinking in my mind. Therefore, I assume that, when another person speaks, his or her words are similarly the product of mental activity.

From Ryle's point of view there is no problem. There is no 'ghost in the machine' – what we mean by mind is the intelligent and communicative abilities of the other person. If I know his or her actions, words, etc. – then I know his or her mind; the two things are one and the same.

Returning to an earlier question:

What is the difference between an actor playing the part of a person in pain, and someone who is actually in pain?

If I say that one really feels pain, while the other only appears to feel pain, do I not assume some non-physical self existing over and above the actual grimaces and moans that lead me to describe the person as being in pain.

But is it possible to know another mind directly? What about telepathy? An experiment carried out by Dr Jacobo Grindberg of the National University of Mexico, was outlined at a conference on science and consciousness in January 1994:

He took a number of couples, some of whom had been in long-term relationships, others who had more recently fallen in love, and had them look into one another's eyes without speaking or touching one another. Then they were separated and put in Faraday cages (which isolates them from external stimuli), and wired up with a device to measure electrical activity of the brain. When a stimulus was applied to one of the subjects, the other mirrored his or her brain activity – even though they could have had no knowledge of the stimulus being applied to the other. Grinberg found that this 'transferred potential' did not diminish, even when the couples were separated by a greater distance, suggesting that the information was not being conveyed by any conventional means.

Commenting on these experiments, Dr Fenwick of the Maudsley Hospital, London, whilst accepting the unlikely possibilities of the experiment not being set up properly or of the results being falsified, added:

> 'The third possibility is that it is a true effect and it comes about in a way we can't account for at present. If you get direct brain-to-brain transfer of physiological stimuli, it seems logical to postulate that the mind may not be entirely confined to the skull.'
>
> (*Sunday Times* 30 January 1994, p.28)

That is certainly one possibility. Another is that, although the mind is directly linked to the brain, and enclosed within the skull, it can communicate with other minds in a way that science cannot yet explain.

This would get round the problem of conceiving a mind that is not limited to the brain – it can carry out many of the functions required by the dualist, merely by communicating with other minds. The one thing it would not be able to do, however, is to survive the death of the brain.

IN OTHER WORDS:

Other minds can be known:

- by observing bodies (so, e.g. Ryle);
- by analogy with myself (the dualist's position);
- because of the phenomenon of language (how could there be communication, unless there were minds with which to communicate);
- by telepathy (if this is accepted as a proven phenomenon).

Is there anything special about knowledge of oneself?

We are immediately aware of our own thoughts. The thoughts of others come to us via their words, gestures and appearance. This has led some people to argue that we can only know our own mind, and we are therefore radically alone, surrounded only by bodies in which we have to infer that there are other minds similar to our own. This is termed 'solipsism', and is the fate of those who think of the soul or mind as a crude, unknowable 'ghost' – the caricature that Ryle presented.

In practice, we get to know other people by observation, by considering what they say or write, and by judging how they deal with life. We can question them, in order to clarify their likes and dislikes, for example. But in the end, we still depend upon our own observation.

An example:

I ask someone, whom I have invited to dinner that evening, if he likes strawberries. He replies that he does.

- If he is telling the truth, and I believe him, then I know at least one think about his own private tastes.
- On the other hand, he could be saying that he likes them in order to be polite (seeing that I am returning home with a punnet of strawberries in my hand when I ask him the question). I need to ask myself if, in my past experience of him, he is someone who is straightforward about his views, or if he is always anxious to please and agree with people. If the latter is the case, then I am really no nearer knowing if he really does like strawberries.
- I could observe him at the dinner table that evening. Does he savour the strawberries, or swallow them quickly? Does he appear to be enjoying himself, or does he suddenly turn rather pale and excuse himself from the table?
- Do I subsequently observe him buying and eating strawberries?

This is a simple example of weighing up the evidence for a person's private sensations. It would become far more complex if the question were 'Did you have a happy childhood?' In this case, there are profound psychological reasons why the immediate response may not be the correct one. Indeed, such is the way in which the unconscious mind affects the conscious, that the person may not actually know if he was or was not happy. Moments of trauma may have been blocked off and unacknowledged. The whole process of psychotherapy is one of gradually unpicking the things that a person says, coupled with their actual behaviour and physical responses.

Knowledge of other minds is therefore a process of assessment, based on observation. It is not instantaneous (If it were, most therapists would starve!). It is constantly open for revision.

I meet up with a friend whom I have not seen for twenty years.

- Do I now treat this senior executive as though he were still the scruffy fifteen year old I once knew, with unchanged tastes and habits? If so, we are unlikely to renew our friendship!

- I have to learn anew – check what remains of old views, check what has changed, ask about life's experiences and their impact.

Notice the assumption that I make in all this – that I am getting to know another person as a communicating subject. I do not explore his brain, nor seek for any occult 'soul'. I simply recognise that he is a person who has views, feelings, thoughts, experiences, and that he can communicate them. That process of communication means that getting to know another person is a two-way process. It depends upon my observation and enquiries, but it also depends upon the willingness of the other person to be known. Without the person's cooperation, even a very experienced psychotherapist would find it extremely difficult to get to know an individual's mind. You can build up a profile – this sort of person with those sort of interests – but not an actual unique individual. Psychologists advising the police can suggest the sort of person who might have committed a particular crime, based on their experience of similar people, especially in the case of those with severe mental disturbance. But they cannot point to a particular individual.

Contrast this with knowledge of yourself:

- It is instantaneous. As soon as I stop to reflect, I can say if I feel happy or not.
- It is based on sensation, not observation I do not have to listen to my own words, or look at my facial expressions in a mirror in order to know if I am enjoying myself. I have immediate sensations of pleasure or pain.

But
- It is not certain. Although my knowledge of myself is more reliable than the knowledge of anyone else, I may still be mistaken. If it were not so, we could never become confused about ourselves, for we would know and understand both our experiences and our responses to them. Adolescence would be negotiated smoothly, mid-life crises would not occur, psychotherapists and counsellors would become extinct. Alas, the process of knowing oneself is probably more complex than knowing another person.

In knowing myself, I have two advantages over others:

1. I have memory. This means that my own knowledge of events and my response to them is more immediate and detailed than the accounts given by others, although my memory may let me down, and (in the case of traumatic experiences) things may be repressed because they are too painful to remember. In such a case, for

example of trauma in childhood, another person may have a clearer memory of what happened and of my response at the time than I have myself.

2. I can deliberately mislead others about my feelings and responses. Generally speaking, except for cases of strong unconscious motivation, I do not mislead myself.

Personal identity

There are many ways of identifying yourself:

- son or daughter of ..... ;
- a member of a particular school, university, business;
- a citizen of a country, member of a race;
- an earthling (if you happen to be travelling through space, this might become a very relevant way of describing yourself).

At various times, each of these will become more or less relevant for the purpose of self-identity.

An example:

Walking down a street in London, I am not likely to think of myself first and foremost as British (unless of course, I am near a famous building, and am surrounded by foreign tourists). Yet if I travel to a far flung and inaccessible part of the globe, I might well say 'I'm British' as one of the first means of identifying myself.

- In general, self-identification is made easier by emphasising those things by which one differs from others around one at the time.
- Those who are fearful of having their individuality exposed, tend to 'blend in' with a crowd – giving themselves an 'identity' in terms of shared values. In practice, this leads to group identity, not individual identity.

In practice, identity is not a matter of body or mind only, but of an integrated functioning entity comprising both body and mind. Of course, once the process of analysis starts, it is difficult to find a 'self' that is not at the same time something else – but that is exactly the reason why identity is not a matter of analysis.

- Analysis shows bits and pieces – none of which are 'you'.
- Synthesis shows the way in which body, mind and social function all come together in a unique combination – and that is 'you'.

Identity is therefore a matter of synthesis, not of analysis. You are the sum total, not the parts.

For reflection:

- Are your thoughts physically contained within your head, even if they originate in brain activity?

- Where are your friendships located? In your head? In the heads of your friends? Somewhere is space between the two? In a level of reality that does not depend on space – if there is such a thing?

- Think of a chat show on radio. The programme is put together by a team of people, it is broadcast across hundreds, perhaps thousands of miles. The words of the host spark off thoughts in the minds of thousands of listeners. Some respond and phone in to the programme. Where is all this located? If there is no physical location for it, what does that say about personal identity and personal communication?

More than once in this chapter we have turned to the idea of an actor, and the distinction between acting and reality. This is also relevant for an understanding of 'persons'. For example, Aldo Tassi, writing in *Philosophy Today* (Summer 1993) explored the idea of a persona or mask that an actor puts on. The actor projects a sense of self – the self who is the character in the play. In doing so the actor withdraws his own identity. In the theatre, the actor can go off stage and revert to his own identity. In the real world, Tassi argues, we create a character in what we do, but we can never step outside the world to find another self 'off stage'. He refers back to Aristotle, for whom the soul is the substantial form of the body, but substance for Aristotle was not a static thing. The soul is not super-added to the body to make it a living thing – rather the body gets both its being and its life from the 'soul'. Tassi says: 'Consciously to be is to project a sense of oneself, that is to say, to "assume a mask"'. (*Philosophy Today* 37:2 p.207)

Personal identity, if Tassi is right, is a dynamic rather than static thing – it is acted out and developed. It does not exist in terms of static analysis.

FOR REFLECTION:

Frankenstein's monster takes on character as the novel unfolds. It is not there latent in the 'materials' with which he starts.

There is much that can be explored in terms of 'persons'. In recent philosophy this has been brought to particular attention by the work of P F Strawson (in 'Persons', an article first published in 1958, and *Individuals*, 1959) who argued that the concept of 'person' was prior to and need not be analysed as an animated body, or embodied mind. Rather, a person is such that both physical characteristics and states of consciousness can be ascribed to it. The concept of a 'person' has many practical and ethical implications:

- In what sense, and at what point, can an unborn child be called a person?
- An unborn child has a brain, but cannot communicate directly. Is such communication necessary for it to be called a full human being? (Consider also the case of the severely handicapped – does lack of communication detract from their being termed 'people'.)
- Does a baby have to be independent before being classified as a person? If so, do we cease to be human once we are rendered totally dependent on others, e.g. on the operating table?
- What is the status of a person who goes into a coma?

Morality therefore depends on a sense of personal identity, and such implications need to be taken into account.

Memory

If you feel pain, you may well do things to show it. These, as we have seen, can sometimes be taken to be the real meaning of having a pain. But with memory it is different. You can remember something without giving any external sign of what you have remembered. Memories are personal, and they are also influential. You are what you are because you have learned from the past, and that learning depends on memory.

A person who has lost his or her memory finds it difficult to function, is constantly surprised or bewildered by the responses of other who claim long-established friendship or hatred. Our responses are determined by our memories.

Hume saw memories as a set of private images running through one's head. It follows that, if I say I have a memory of a particular thing, nobody else can contradict me, because nobody else has access to that particular bit of internal data. But what if one thinks that one remembers something and then is shown that it would not be possible, e.g. that I remember the Second World War, only to find that I was born after it was over. I would have to admit that my memory was faulty, or perhaps that a war film had lodged such vivid images in my mind that I genuinely believed that I had lived through it. I remember the image clearly enough, and am not lying about it, but what I have forgotten is the origin of that image, the original experience (on film, in this case, and not reality).

Memory errors can sometimes be countered by the idea that the person imagined an event rather than remembered it – again, there is no doubting the mental image, what is at doubt is the origin of the image.

Arguments about the nature of memory tend to be based on language. What does it mean to say that I have remembered something? Does it make sense to say that I have remembered my name every time I go to sign something? Clearly, there is a difference between the body of information (from remembering my name and address to knowing that $2 \times 2 = 4$) to remembering particular events, "Where were you on the night of August the second, at the time when the murder was committed?"

Great feats of memory require sifting below the many facts and images that are habitually available to us, to more specific events – remembering a place leads to remembering a particular person who was seen there, leads to remembering any suspicious actions that he or she may have made. The feature of such memory is that it is revealed bit by bit – or, sometimes, that something previously forgotten is triggered. Following serious crimes, an identically dressed person is sometimes sent to retrace the steps of the victim, hoping that it may trigger off a memory in a passer-by.

Memories are thus private; only we have them. But they are also public in that they are frequently of events, people, or information which is in the public domain and may therefore form the basis of other people's memories. But just because we may have privileged access to our own memories, does not mean that we are infallible. Four people giving accounts of a dinner party may all provide quite different versions of events. Our memories are selective, providing us with recall of those sense experiences which are deemed significant, and ignoring those that are not.

Memory also serves to develop the 'background' of our actions and thoughts (to use Heidegger's term) – through memory, I gather the general information about the world which is what enables me to think, evaluate and act.

IN OTHER WORDS:

The mind/body problem is important for philosophy because:

- Thinking is a mental activity. Doing philosophy implies a relationship between the mind and the world of the senses.
- It touches on many other areas: epistemology (How do we know minds?); metaphysics (Is mind reducible to matter, or matter to mind?); the language we use to describe intelligent life.
- Because it has to do with persons, it is relevant to issues of morality.

———— A 'personal' postscript ————

The mind/body issue, perhaps more than any other, illustrates the problem of the analytic and reductionist approach to complex entities. Frankenstein got it wrong! The analysis and reassembling of the components of a human being – whether it be a crude autopsy to hunt for the elusive 'soul', or the sophisticated attempt to reproduce the process of thinking with the aid of computers, is, I am convinced, unlikely to produce more than a caricature of a human person.

The experience of being a thinking, feeling and reflecting person, is not susceptible to analysis because it is not part of the world as we experience it. Wittgenstein was right in saying that the self was the limit of the world, rather than part of it.

Nor is the self a fixed entity. Hume could never see his mind except by

the procession of thoughts that passed through it. From birth to
there is constant change, and our thoughts of today shape what w
shall be tomorrow.

Throughout life, however, we leave our imprint on the world around
us: words we speak, actions we perform, roles we assume. It is these
that form our changing story, these that define our character from
moment to moment.

Even our process of reflection, the most private of activities, is dependent
upon the outside world. It is extremely difficult to experience something
with absolute simplicity, for we immediately categorise it – our patterns
of thinking shaped by common language and culture.

Philosophers and scientists tend to think, to search around in the
mental jungle for ideas, concepts, theories and evidence. Hence their
problem in locating the self. By contrast, those who practise meditation,
who still the mind until it is gently focused on a single point, become
aware of something very different. The self becomes empty, becomes
nothing and everything at the same moment. There is no self. Returning
to the world of everyday experience, the self continues its ever-
changing patterns of thought, feeling and response – we can but watch
and enjoy its kaleidoscope.

4

THE PHILOSOPHY OF SCIENCE

The philosophy of science examines the methods used by science, the ways in which hypotheses and laws are formulated from evidence, and the grounds on which scientific claims about the world may be justified.

Philosophy and science are not in principle opposed to one another, but are in many ways parallel operations, for both seek to understand the nature of the world and its structures. Whereas the individual sciences do so by gathering data from within their particular spheres and formulating general theories for understanding them, philosophy tends to concern itself with the process of formulating principles, and establishing how they relate together into an overall view. We saw in chapter one that metaphysics is the task of understanding the basic structures of reality that lie behind all the findings of individual sciences.

A major part of all philosophy is the process of analysing the language people use and the criteria of truth that they accept. While the individual sciences use 'first order language' (speaking directly about physical, chemical or biological observations), philosophy uses 'second order language' (examining what it means to speak about those things). It does this by looking at what is said, and whether or not the language used accurately reflects the reality which it purports to describe. (We saw in the last chapter that Ryle examined the description of mental operations, and argued that the 'ghost in the machine' idea of the mind was not required by that language.)

Today, scientists tend to work in specialised fields – a particular branch of physics, for example – because it is quite impossible for anyone to have the sort of detailed knowledge of the current state of research in all the various aspects of science. Scientists, mathematicians and philosophers may therefore be seen today as working in different disciplines, even if each is interested in and may benefit from the work of the others. It was not always so, and physics was originally known as 'Natural Philosophy'. What is more, some of the greatest names in philosophy were involved with mathematics and science:

Aristotle examined and codified the various sciences, and did so within his overall scheme of philosophy. Descartes, Leibniz, Pascal and Russell were all mathematicians as well as philosophers. (Indeed, Russell and Whitehead argued in *Principia Mathematica* that mathematics was a development of deductive logic.) Bacon, Locke and others were influenced by the rise of modern scientific method, and were concerned to give it a sound philosophical basis. Kant wrote *A General Natural History and Theory of the Heavens* in 1755, in which he explored the possible origin of the solar system. Some philosophical movements (e.g. logical positivism, in the early years of the twentieth century) were influenced by science and the scientific method of establishing evidence. Many of the philosophers that we considered in the chapter on the theory of knowledge can therefore re-appear in considering science – largely because scientific knowledge and its methods are such an important part of our general appreciation of the scope and method of human knowledge.

In order to put these things into perspective, however, we shall take a brief historical look at some of the philosophers who commented on science, or were influenced by it.

———— An historical overview ————

Within Western thought there have been two major shifts in the view of the world, and these have had an important influence on the way in which philosophy and science have related to one another. We may therefore divide Western philosophy of science into three general periods: early Greek and Medieval thought; the Newtonian world-view; twentieth-century science (although recognising that such division represents the simplification of a more complex process of change).

Early Greek and Medieval thought

In 529CE Emperor Justinian banned the teaching of philosophy in order to further the interests of Christianity. Plato had already had a considerable influence upon the development of Christian doctrines, and elements of his thought – particularly the contrast between the ideal world of the forms and the limited world of everyday experience – continued within theology. The works of Aristotle were preserved first in Byzantium and then by the Arabs, being re-discovered only in the thirteenth century, when the first translations were made from Arabic into Latin.

It is only from the thirteenth century, therefore, with thinkers like Thomas Aquinas (1225-74), Duns Scotus (1266-1308) and William of Ockham (c1285-1349), that Greek thought began to be explored again in a systematic way. From that time, philosophy is very much a development of, or reaction to, the work of the Greeks. It is only with Descartes (see p.19) that it starts again from first principles, and this coincided with the move into the second phase of science.

Aristotle set out the different branches of science, and divided up living things into their various species and genera – a process of classification which became a major feature of science. He had a theory of knowledge based on sensations which depended on repetition:

sensations repeat themselves...   – leading to perception
perceptions repeat themselves...   – leading to experience
experiences repeat themselves...   – leading to knowledge

Therefore we find that knowledge is something that develops out of our structured perception and experience of the material that comes to us from our senses – an important feature of the philosophy of science.

He also established ideas of space, time and causality, including the idea of the 'Prime Mover' (which became the basis of the cosmological argument for the existence of God – see p56). He distinguished between the four 'causes' (see above p31), thus distinguishing between matter and the form it took on, the agent of change and the final purpose or goal for which something was designed. He considered a thing's power to be its potential. Each thing had a potential and a resting place – fire will, by nature, rise, whereas heavy objects will fall. Changes, for Aristotle, are not related to general forces like gravity (which belong to the later Newtonian scheme), but to the fact that individual things, by their very nature, seek to follow their nature.

Let us look at a few examples of the influence of Plato and Aristotle:

For Plato, the unseen 'forms' were more real than the individual things that could be known through the senses. This way of thinking (backed by religion) led to the idea that reason and the concepts of perfection could determine what existed, and that any observations which appeared to contradict this must automatically be wrong.

Cosmology and astronomy give examples of this: Copernicus (1473-1543) and later Galileo (1564-1642) were to offer a view of the universe in which the Earth revolved around the Sun, rather than vice versa. Their view was opposed by those whose idea of the universe came from Ptolemy and in which the Earth was surrounded by glassy spheres – perfect shapes, conveying the Sun, Moon, planets in perfect circular motion. Their work was challenged (and Galileo condemned) not because their observations were found to be at fault, but because they had trusted their observations, rather than deciding beforehand what should be the case. Kepler (1571-1630) concluded that the orbit of Mars was elliptical, whereas all heavenly motion was thought to be perfect, and therefore circular.

These astronomers were struggling against a background of religious authority which gave Greek notions of perfection priority over observations and experimental evidence. In other words, the earlier medieval system of thought was 'deductive' – it deduced what should happen from its ideas, in contrast to the later 'inductive' method of getting to a theory from observations.

Along with the tendency to look for theory and perfection rather than observation, there was another, stemming from Aristotle. Following his idea of the final cause, everything was thought to be designed for a particular purpose. If something falls to the ground, it seeks its natural purpose and place in doing so. So, in a religious context, it was possible to say that something happened because it was God's will for it, or because it was designed for that purpose. There was no need to look for a scientific principle or law which would apply to everything without distinction.

The Newtonian world-view

The rise of modern science would not have been possible without the renewed sense of the value of human reason and the ability to challenge established ideas and religious dogma, which developed as a result of the Renaissance and the Reformation. But what was equally influential was the way in which information was gathered and sorted, and theories formed on the basis of it. Central to this process was the method of 'induction', and this was set out very clearly (and in a way that continues to be relevant) by Francis Bacon.

Bacon (1561-1626) rejected Aristotle's idea of final causes, and insisted that knowledge should be based on a process of induction, which, as we shall see later, is the systematic method of coming to general conclusions on the basis of evidence about individual instances that have been observed. He warned about 'idols': those things that tend to lead a person astray. They included:

- the desire to accept that which confirms what we already believe;
- distortions resulting from our habitual ways of thinking;
- muddles that come through our use of language (e.g. using the same word for different things, and then assuming that they must be one and the same);
- believing things out of allegiance to a particular school of thought.

Bacon also pointed out that, in gathering evidence, one should not just seek those examples that would confirm a particular theory, but should actively seek out and accept the force of contrary examples. After centuries of using evidence to confirm what was already known by dogma or reason, this was quite revolutionary.

The general view of the world which came about as a result of the rise of science is usually linked with the name of Isaac Newton (1642-1727). In the Newtonian world-view, observation and experiment yield knowledge of the laws which governed the whole world. In it, space and time were fixed, forming a framework within which everything takes place. Objects were seen to move and be moved through the operation of physical laws of motion, so that everything was seen as a machine, the workings of which could become known through careful observation. Interlocking forces kept matter in motion, and everything was predictable. Not everything might be known at this moment, but there was no doubt that everything would be understood eventually, using the established scientific method.

Put crudely, the world was largely seen as a collection of particles of matter in motion – hitting one another, like billiard balls on a table, and behaving in a predictable way. It was thought that science would eventually give an unchallengeable explanation for everything, and that it would form the basis for technology that would give humankind increasing control over the environment, and the ability to do things as yet unimagined. Science became cumulative – gradually expanding into previously unknown areas; building upon the secure foundations of established physical laws.

Newton was a religious believer; he thought that the laws by which the universe operated had been established by God. But his god was an external creator who, once the universe had been set in motion, could retire, leaving it to continue to function according to its fixed laws. This view freed science from the need to take God into account: it could base its theories on observation rather than religious dogma.

With the coming of the Newtonian world-view, the function of philosophy changed. Rather than initiating theories about cosmology, the task of philosophy was to examine and comment on the methods and results of scientific method, establishing its limits. It also pointed out, through Kant, that the laws of nature (indeed, space, time and causality – the very bases of Newtonian science) were not to be found 'out there' in the world of independent objects, but were contributed by the mind.

Hume pointed out that scientific laws were not true universal statements, but only summaries of what had been experienced so far. The very method used – gathering data and drawing general conclusions from it – yielded higher and higher degrees of probability, but there was no way of moving from this to absolute certainty.

Some aspects of philosophy related to this phase of science have already been examined (in chapter 1). Hume's empiricism, for example, fits perfectly with the scientific impetus. At the beginning of the nineteenth century William Paley's argument in favour of a designer for the universe (see p.58) reflects the domination of his world view by the paradigm of the machine – a designer (God) is proposed in order to account for the signs of design in creation.

But not all philosophers of this second scientific era supported Newton's fixed mechanical universe. Bishop Berkeley criticised Newton's idea that space and time are fixed. For Berkeley, everything (including matter and extension) is a matter of sensation, of human experience. Thus everything is relative to the person who experiences it, and there is no logical way to move from the relativity of our experience to some external absolute. In his own way, Berkeley anticipates the arrival of the third era for science and philosophy.

Twentieth-century science

For most thinkers prior to the twentieth century, it was inconceivable that space and time were not fixed: a necessary framework within which everything else could take place.

Einstein's theories of relativity were to change all that. The first, in 1905, was the theory of 'Special Relativity', best known in the form of the equation $E=mc^2$. This showed that mass and energy are equivalent, and that (since energy was equal to mass multiplied by the speed of light squared) a very small amount of matter could be converted into a very large amount of energy. This, of course, is now best known for its rather drastic practical consequences in the development of nuclear weapons.

Einstein published the second theory, 'General Relativity', in 1916. It made the revolutionary claim that time, space, matter and energy were all related to one another. For example, space and time can be compressed by a strong gravitational field. There are no fixed points. The way in which things relate to one another depends upon the point from which they are being observed.

An example:

Imagine you are looking out through space. You see two stars, which, although they may appear to you to be at the same distance, are in fact many light years apart. Suppose you see a change in one of those stars, followed by a change in the other. You might reasonably claim that one happened first, because from your perspective they occurred in a time sequence which, on Earth, would amount to one coming first and the other second.

But imagine that you are transported to a star that is beyond the second of the stars that you have been observing. In this case, you would see the second change first and the first change second. Clearly, the reason for this is that the time at which something happens is related to the distance it is from you – because events only come to be observed after the light from them had travelled across space.

It is therefore impossible to say which event happened first; it all depends upon your point of view.

Modern physics and modern cosmology therefore offer a strange view of space and time, a view that is in contrast to that of the Newtonian world. We are told that the whole universe emerged (at the 'big bang') from a space-time singularity – a point at which all the matter of the present universe was concentrated into a very small point. Like a balloon being blown up, space and time expanded as did the universe and, by implication, they are still expanding and changing. The reason Newton's physics worked on the basis of fixed space and time was that he only considered a very small section of the universe, and within that section, his laws do indeed hold true.

Space and time are seen as linked in a single, four-dimensional space-time continuum, and there is no fixed point from which to observe anything, for observer and observed are both in a process of change, moving both through time and through space.

Alongside this came quantum mechanics, which raised questions about whether events at the sub-atomic level could be predicted, and what it means to say that one thing causes another. Matter was no longer thought to be composed of solid atoms, but the atom itself was divided into many constituent particles, held together by forces. In the sub-atomic world, particles did not obey fixed rules. Their individual movements, whilst statistically predictable, were uncertain. Energy was seen to operate by the interchange of little packets or 'quanta', rather than by a single continuous flow. What had once been solid matter obeying fixed mechanical laws, could now be thought of as bundles of events open to a number of different interpretations depending on the viewpoint of the observer. Quantum mechanics is notoriously difficult to understand. A general view of it is that it works, so there must be something right about it, even if we don't understand it as a theory. What is certain is that quantum mechanics, combined with the theories of relativity, rendered the old Newtonian certainties obsolete. Newton's laws of physics might still apply, but only within limited parameters. Once you stray into the microscopic area of the sub-atomic, or the macroscopic world of cosmic structures, the situation is quite different.

A similar revolution has taken place within the understanding of living things. Through the discovery of DNA, the world of biology is linked to that of chemistry and of physics, since the instructions within the DNA molecule are able to determine the form of the living being.

Therefore, in the twentieth century, philosophy engaged with a scientific world and set of ideas that had changed enormously from the mechanical and predictable world of Newton. In particular, science now offers a variety of ways of picturing the world, and cosmology – dominated first by religious belief and Aristotle, then by astronomy – is now very much in the hands of mathematicians. The world as a whole is not something that can be observed, but something the structure of which can be explored by calculation.

During much of the first half of the twentieth century, philosophy (at least in America and Britain) became dominated by the quest for meaning and the analysis of language. It no longer saw its role as providing an overview of the universe – that was left to the individual scientific disciplines. Rather, it adopted a supportive role, checking on the methods used by science, the logic by which results were produced from observations, and the way in which theories could be confirmed or discredited.

IN OTHER WORDS:

- Up to the sixteenth century, Greek concepts, backed by religious authority, determined the general view of the world. Evidence was required to fit the overall scheme.
- In Newtonian physics, matter exists within a fixed structure of space and time, and obeys laws that can be discovered by 'induction' based on observation.
- The modern world-view sees space and time as related to one another, and events as interpreted in the light of the observer's own position and methods of observation.

In the first phase, philosophy seemed to determine **content**, in the second it offered a critique of **method**, and in the third it offers **a clarification of concepts**.

Theory and observation

In terms of the philosophy of science, the most important approach to gathering and analysing information was the 'inductive method'. This was championed by Francis Bacon, and then by Thomas Hobbes (1588-1679) and became the basis of the Newtonian world of science. In its practical approach to sifting and evaluating evidence, it is also reflected in the empiricism of Hume (see p.23). Indeed, it was the inductive method that distinguished 'modern' science from what had gone before, and brought in the first of the two major shifts in world view.

The inductive method

This method is based on two things:

1. The trust that knowledge can be gained by gathering evidence and conducting experiments, i.e. it is based on facts that can be checked, or experiments that can be repeated.
2. The willingness to set aside preconceived views about the likely outcome of an experiment, or the validity of evidence presented, i.e. the person using this method does not have a fixed idea about its conclusion, but is open to examine both results and methods used with an open mind.

With the inductive method, science was claiming to be based on facts and on open-mindedness, and as such was seen as being in contrast to traditional religion, which was seen to be based on doctrines that a person was required to accept and which were backed up by authority rather than reason alone.

In practice, the method works in this way:

- Observe and gather data (evidence; information), seeking to eliminate, as far as possible, all irrelevant factors.
- Analyse your data, and draw conclusions from it in the form of hypotheses.
- Devise experiments to test out those hypotheses. i.e. if this hypothesis is correct, then certain experimental results should be anticipated.
- Modify you hypothesis, if necessary, in the light of the experiments.
- From the experiments, the data and the hypotheses, argue for a theory.
- Once you have a theory, you can predict other things on the basis of it, by which the theory can later be verified or disproved.

It is clear that this process of induction, by which a theory is arrived at by the analysis and testing out of observed data, can yield at most only a high degree of probability. There is always the chance that an additional piece of information will show that the original hypothesis is wrong, or that it only applies within a limited field. The hypothesis, and the scientific theory that comes from it, is therefore open to modification.

Theories that are tested out in this way lead to the framing of scientific laws. Now it is important to establish exactly what is meant by 'law' in this case. In common parlance, 'law' is taken to be something which is imposed, a rule that is to be obeyed. But it would be wrong to assume that a scientific law can dictate how things behave. The law simply describes that behaviour, it does not control it (as Hume argued). If something behaves differently, it is not to be blamed for going against a law of nature, it is simply that either:

- there is an unknown factor that has influenced this particular situation and therefore modified what was expected, or
- the law of nature is inadequately framed, and needs to be modified in order to take this new situation into account.

A most influential thinker on this was Karl Popper (1902-1994). In his book *The Logic of Scientific Discovery* (1934, trans.1959) he makes the important point that science seeks theories that are logically self-consistent, and that can be falsified. Now he points out that a scientific law goes beyond what can be experienced. We can never absolutely prove it to be true, all we can do is try to prove it to be false, and accept it on a provisional basis until such time as it is falsified in this way.

This leads Popper to say that a scientific theory cannot be compatible with all the logically possible evidence that could be considered. It must be possible to falsify it. If a theory claims that it can never be falsified, then it is not scientific.

In practice, of course, a theory is not automatically discarded as soon as one possible piece of contrary evidence is produced. What happens is that the scientist tries to reproduce that bit of contrary evidence, to show that it is part of a significant pattern that the theory has not been able to account for. Science also seeks out alternative theories that can include all the positive evidence that has been found for the original one, but also includes the new conflicting evidence.

An example:

In Newtonian physics, light travels in a straight line. (This was confirmed over the centuries, and was therefore corroborated as a theory.)

But modern astronomy has shown that, when near to a very

---

powerful gravitational field, light bends.

This does **not** mean that the Newtonian view was wrong, simply that light does indeed travel in a straight line when in a uniform gravitational field. The older theory is now included within a new one which can take into account these exceptional circumstances.

Where you have a choice of theories, Popper held that you should accept the one that is better corroborated than the others, more testable, and entails more true statements than the others. And that you should do this, even if you know that the theory is false! The implication of this would seem to be that science takes a pragmatic rather than an absolute approach to truth. Since we anyway cannot have absolute certainty, we have to go for the most useful way of understanding the world that we have to hand, even if its limitations have already been revealed.

IN OTHER WORDS:

- I observe that Y follows X on a number of occasions.
- On the basis of this I put forward the hypothesis that X is the cause of Y.
- I make further tests, and on each occasion Y follows X.
- I therefore formulate a scientific law to the effect that X is the cause of Y, meaning that Y will always follow X.
- **But** I can't know that for certain. I can't check out every possible example of X.
- **Therefore** it doesn't make the law any more secure to keep multiplying the number of positive results that I get. To test out the law, what I really need is a negative result. I need just a single example of an X which is not followed by a Y in order to show that the law is wrong and needs modification or replacement.

—— What difference do we make? ——

Karl Popper argued that science was not subjective, in the sense of being the product of a single human mind, but neither was it literally objective (i.e. a scientific law is not an external 'fact', but a way of stating the relationship between facts as they appear to us). Rather, it transcends the ideas of individuals, as does art, literature or maths. But exactly what sort of difference do we make to our perception of the world?

The process of induction is based on the idea that it is possible to get hard evidence which does not depend upon the person who observes it. A scientist sets aside all personal preferences in assessing data. Thus the resulting theory is meant to apply to all people at all times. But can we observe nature without influencing it by our act of observing it, and how much of what we think of as evidence is contributed by our own minds?

The sensations that we have are not simply copies of external reality, they are the product of the way in which we have encountered that reality: colour is the result of a combination of light, surface texture and the operation of our eyes; space is perceived as a result of our brain linking one thing to another; time is a matter of remembering that some experiences have already taken place. Scientific theories are therefore not based on independent facts, but are the product of our ways of looking and thinking.

Kant argued that when we observe something, our mind has a contribution to make to that experience. Space, time and causality are all imposed on experience by the mind in order to make sense of it. Physics since Einstein has endorsed this relevance of the observer for an understanding of what it observed. As we saw above, neither space nor time is fixed, and movement is only perceived in terms of the change in position of one body in relation to another.

Example:

I look out of the window of a stationary train at the train in the next platform. Suddenly, what I see starts to move. But is my train moving forward, or is the *other* train pulling away? Unless I feel a jolt, it will be a moment before I can decide between the two – and I will only be able to do so by looking beyond or away from the other train to some third object.

Following Popper, and also following ideas considered in the first chapter in connection with epistemology in general, we see that what is perceived may be understood to transcend the individual perceiver simply because that perception is shared. Several people all witnessing the existence of a table in the room will confirm my own perception. In the same way, scientific evidence, repeated in various experiments, gives a trans-personal element of truth, even if the object being studied, and the way in which it is described, ultimately depend upon human perceptions. We do indeed make a difference, but science can take account of those differences.

————— New evidence? —————

A theory which may be deemed inadequate on the basis of lack of evidence, may find that subsequent evidence of a very different kind can make it again a theory of choice. In this way, a theory survives when it adapt to new situations yielding new evidence. Theories may have to adapt in order to survive ... a kind of natural selection in the scientific world.

A particularly appropriate example of this may be Charles Darwin's theory of natural selection. Darwin published *The Origin of Species* in 1859. He put forward his theory that species could gradually evolve through the selective passing of qualities to successive generations by those members of a species who were able to survive and breed. This was not a moral theory, but an intuitive grasp of a process that he considered the best explanation for the variety of species that he observed.

The basic facts are difficult to challenge. Those who survive into adulthood, do in fact breed. Those species that adapt to a particular environment thrive there. Such evidence leads to a hypothesis which becomes the basis for a theory which claims to explain changes that span millennia.

By thus following the inductive method, Darwin claimed to have discovered the mechanism by which species evolve, and also an explanation of those features of each species which seem most appropriate to its own survival. The inductive method has therefore, so it seemed, replaced ideas of design (see p.58).

The debates that followed the publication of Darwin's theory were not simply about his perceived challenge to religious ideas, but about his interpretation of evidence. In particular, there did not seem to be adequate fossil evidence for a gradual transition from one species to another. And, of course, weighing such evidence was an essential feature of the inductive method.

COMMENT:

Perhaps the theory of natural selection represents a halfway house between a strict inductive method of scientific argument and the sort of imaginative leap from a limited experience to a more general theory.

Darwin did gather a great deal of evidence, but the debates that followed were sparked by the recognition that, if such a theory of evolution was correct, then its implications were far beyond his areas of research. If species are not fixed, then everything is subject to change. To accept such an idea (with all its scientific, social, emotional and religious implications) on the basis of limited evidence was to take a great risk.

The basis upon which a theory is examined may change over a period of time. One of the major criticisms of Darwin's theory of evolution was the lack of fossil evidence for the 'half-way' stages of change from what appeared to be one fixed species to another. Since many of those who wish to challenge Darwin's theory do so for religious reasons, their concern is with origins, and they therefore tend to look to the past.

In fact, further evidence for the general validity of Darwin's approach now comes from the present. A book entitled *The Beak of the Finch*, by Jonathan Weiner (Cape, 1994) describes a twenty-year study of finches on one of the Galapagos Islands, showing, for example, that in times of drought only those finches with the longest beaks could succeed in getting the toughest seeds, and therefore survived to breed. At the same time, DNA studies of blood from various finches corresponded to their physical abilities and characteristics.

More generally, evidence for survival of the fittest is seen all the time in terms of medicine and agriculture. As soon as a pesticide appears to have brought a particular pest under control, a new strain is found which is resistant to it. Equally, in medicine, new strains of disease are appearing which are resistant to the available antibiotics. What is happening is that those examples of a pest or a disease which survive the onslaught of a pesticide or treatment, breed. The next generation is therefore resistant. These examples show the flexibility of nature: the present disease has been 'designed', not by some original designer but in response to existing treatments. We see an evolution of species and diseases over a space of a few years, mirroring the longer term evolution over millennia.

There is no way that Darwin could have considered his theory from the standpoint of genetic mutation, or from the way in which viruses adapt and take on new forms, but that new area of evidence may be used to corroborate a previously held theory, particularly where (as was the case with Darwin) the problem was not so much that his theory had been falsified as that there was a perceived lack of positive evidence.

——— Right, wrong or what? ———

The Newtonian world was at least predictable. A law of nature could be regarded as a fixed piece of information about how the world worked. That has now gone. We find that science can offer equally valid but different ways of viewing the same phenomenon. There are no absolutes of space or time. Quantum theory is seen to work (results can be predicted on the basis of it), but without people understanding exactly why.

An example:

Light can be understood in terms of particles or in terms of wave motions. They are two utterly different ways of understanding the same thing, but the fact that one is right does not mean that the other is wrong.

As laws and theories become established within the scientific community, they are used as a basis for further research, and are termed 'paradigms'. Occasionally there is a paradigm shift, which entails the revision of much of science. In terms of cosmology, the move from an Aristotelian (Ptolemaic) to a Newtonian world-view, and then the further move from that to the view of Einstein, represents two shifts of paradigm.

At any one time, therefore, science offers a set of reasoned views about how the world has been seen to work up to the present. Taken together, the laws of science that are understood at any one time provide a structure within which scientists work, a structure which guides, influences but does not dictate how scientific research will progress. With hindsight we can see philosophers and scientists boldly proclaiming the finality of their particular vision of the world, just as the scientific community is about to go through a 'paradigm shift' as a result of which everything is re-examined.

An example:

In 1899, Haeckel published *The Riddle of the Universe*. He argued that everything, including thought, was the product of material world and was controlled by its laws. Everything was absolutely controlled and determined. Freedom was an illusion and religion a superstition. He was proposing scientific materialism, popularising Darwin's theory of evolution, and sweeping away all earlier philosophy which did not fit his material and scientific outlook. What would Haeckel have made of relativity and quantum theory?

T S Kuhn, in his book *The Structure of Scientific Revolutions* (Chicago, 1962), described these 'paradigms' as the basic Gestalt (or world-view) within which science at any one time interprets the evidence it has available. It is the paradigm that largely dictates scientific progress, and observations are not free from the influence of the paradigm.

Since there is no independent data, science, according to Kuhn, debates between competing paradigms. This implies a relativism in science. If a theory works well, if it gives good predictive results, then it becomes a possible explanation. We cannot say that it is the definitive or only one.

IN OTHER WORDS:

- Different theories can give an equally true explanation of the same phenomenon.
- A scientific theory is a way of looking: a convenient way of organising experience, but not necessarily the only one. It is provisional. It is part of an overall paradigm.

Does that make any one scientific theory right, wrong or what? This is a question for the philosophy of science: Can we say that something is 'right' in a world of optional viewpoints?

—— What counts as science? ——

An activity is generally called 'scientific' if it followed the inductive method. On these grounds, the work of Marx could be called scientific in that he based his theories on accounts of political changes in the societies he studied. Similarly, a behavioural psychologist can claim to be scientific on the basis of the methods used: observing and recording the responses of people and animals to particular stimuli. So science is defined by method rather than by subject.

An example:

Astronomy is regarded as a science. Astrology, on the other hand, is not. This is because the former is based on observable facts, whilst the latter is based on a mythological scheme.

Except: suppose astrologers could show that there was a definite link between a person's star sign and his or her behaviour. Suppose the results of a very large number of studies indicated this. Would that constitute evidence?

On the face of it, it would probably depend upon who did the experiment; if it were an attempt to gather favourable information to support the previously held views, then it would not be acceptable. On the other hand, if it were gathered in a strictly objective way, by someone who genuinely wanted to know if the phenomena of star signs was relevant to human behaviour, then it might be claimed to be scientific.

Then, even if this were regarded as a scientific basis for astrology, it would only be termed a science if its practitioners subsequently appeared to be using scientific methods of assessment and prediction.

Distinguishing features of the science include the consistent attempt at the disinterested gathering of information and the willingness to accept revision of one's theories. But what happens if one's conclusions are radically different from those of other scientists?

—— Heretics, orthodox and vested —— Interests

With the rise of science in the seventeenth and eighteenth centuries, it was widely believed that the days of superstition and authority were over; everything was to be considered rationally. But has that always remained the case with science?

Once a theory, or a method of working, has become established, the scientific world tends to treat it as the norm and to be rather suspicious of any attempt to follow a radically different approach. When Darwin introduced the idea of natural selection or Einstein that of relativity, the radical changes in scientific outlook that they implied were seen by some as a threat to the steady accumulating of knowledge along the previously accepted ways of seeing the world. Although both were accepted, there was a pause for consideration.

Today there are many scientists who are held to be 'heretics' within the world of scientific orthodoxy; people whose views are so much at variance with the scientific norm that their views are often discounted.

Since we have seen that there can be several different ways of approaching a single phenomenon, and that they can be simultaneously and equally valid, there will always be an element of debate within scientific circles. Controversies arise where a theory does not seem to fit the established paradigm. Some views are dismissed by a majority of scientists simply because there is not sufficient evidence offered to warrant a radical re-evaluation of present views.

An example:

The chemist Linus Pauling claimed that Vitamin C was a panacea that could not only prevent colds, but could help resist cancer and prevent heart disease. In spite of the recognition of his work on molecular structures, for which he had received a Nobel Prize, his views on this were generally dismissed by the scientific community, although they became popular with the general public.

Other theories, once publicised, are evaluated by other scientists. The original experiments are repeated elsewhere to see if the same results can be obtained, since if something is true, it should be repeatable.

Sometimes the results of attempting this are ambiguous; sometimes the attempt to repeat the experiment failed completely, and the validity and reliability of the original results are therefore called into question.

An example:

The American physicists Fleischmann and Pons put forward the claim that they had achieved a breakthrough in the quest for cold nuclear fission – the possibility of creating unlimited supplies of energy by creating nuclear fission under normal laboratory circumstances. (Generally, nuclear fission can only be simulated in the very energy-intensive situations of particle accelerators, and in these circumstances, the energy generated is far, far less than the energy used in the experiment.) Clearly, if it were found that cold nuclear fission were possible, it would revolutionise the human use of energy.

This was received with a degree of scepticism, but their experiments were studied and repeated many times by other scientists. However, they failed to give any positive confirmation. The assumption made was that there must be something wrong with an experiment if its results are so much at variance with existing scientific understanding. However, this is still open for debate, and we may find that cold nuclear fission is possible after all!

Scientists have to earn a living. Some are employed by universities, and, in theory, are free to explore their theories without external influence – other than the requirement that they show real advance in research in order to continue to attract funding. On the other hand, the funding for such research often comes from the commercial world, and is not therefore totally disinterested.

Other scientists are employed within various industries. Their task is to find a scientific basis and make possible the enterprise which their industry seeks to promote. They are not engaged in 'pure' science (in the sense of a quest for knowledge, unfettered by its implications) but science put to the use of industry. Their task is halfway between science and technology – they seek a basis upon which a technology can be developed in order to achieve something that will then yield a profit.

PHILOSOPHY

An example:

A scientist employed by a drugs company is hardly likely to keep his job if his conclusion is that the disease he is attempting to combat by the development of a new drug is best cured by drinking pure fruit juice!

He or she is therefore likely to try the following:

- Isolate the element within the fruit juice which actually effects the cure.

- Synthesise that element under laboratory conditions.

- Enlist technology to manufacture and market that synthesised element in tablet form!

On the other hand, the same scientist might find a suitable post within a company that processes fruit juice.

Increasingly, science is looking for commercial funding. But commercial funding is looking for new products and new ideas for developing those things in which it has a vested interest. Philosophers like Bacon and Hume insisted that the quest for knowledge should be a disinterested one. Indeed, the fact that a scientist stands to gain a great deal from a particular conclusion to his or her research might indicate that the results should be treated with some caution. We have already seen that there are really no facts that are free of interpretation – and this flexibility, coupled with a personal motive, makes the tendency to incline towards the most favourable conclusion a threat to impartiality!

IN OTHER WORDS:

- Philosophy cannot determine what information is available to science: it cannot provide data.
- Philosophy examines the use of scientific data, and the logical processes by which this information can become the basis of scientific theories.
- Most importantly, philosophy can remind scientists that facts always contain an element of interpretation. Facts are the product of a thinking mind encountering external evidence, and they therefore contain both that evidence and the mental framework

by means of which it has been apprehended, and through which it is articulated.

For reflection:

What can be said about the world, and what cannot?

In *Tractatus* Wittgenstein took the view that the function of language was one of picturing the world and started with the bold statement 'The world is everything that is the case.' (*Tractatus* 1.) and equates what can be said with what science can show: 'The totality of true propositions is the whole of natural science.' (*Tractatus* 4.11).

It ends, however, with the admission that when it comes to the mystical (the intuitive sense of the world as a whole) language fails; we must remain silent. What is 'seen' in a moment of mystical awareness cannot be 'pictured'. It cannot be expressed literally.

Wittgenstein points to other things that cannot be described – the subject self (it sees a world, but is not part of that world) and even death (we do not live to experience death). Wittgenstein is thus setting limits to what can be said, and by implication, limits to science.

His thought might prompt us to ask:

- Is not modern cosmology a bit 'mystical'? Does it not seek to find images (including that of the 'big bang') by which to express events so unlike anything experienced of Earth, that literal language is of little use?
- Does science not sometimes require imaginative leaps beyond evidence, in the formation of new paradigms within which detailed work and calculation can subsequently find its place?
- What is the place of intuition in the scientific process? Like an eye which sees everything other than itself, intuition may underpin much of the scientific endeavour without ever itself featuring directly.

Science offers a very rich and exciting view of the world. Whether you start by considering the idea that matter is a collection of nuclear forces, rather than something solid and tangible, or whether you start with the idea that the universe is expanding outwards from the space-time singularity at the 'big bang', creating its own space and time as it does so, modern science seems to contradict our common-sense notions. Yet in doing so it actually shakes us out of our ordinary assumptions, makes us realise that the world is not as simple as it appears. In this, science acts like philosophy: shaking assumptions and examining the basis of what is said.

Yet the impact of science on life is not confined to theoretical knowledge; it has practical consequences. Through the products of technology, science raises ethical issues, from transplants and genetic engineering to nuclear weapons. In this, it comes into contact with another branch of philosophy – ethics – to which we now turn.

5

ETHICS

—— Facts, values and choices ——

So far we have been exploring questions of knowledge: What can we know for certain? Can we know anything about the nature of reality as a whole? How are our language and our thought related to the experiences that come to us through our senses? These led on to three big issues for philosophy: the existence of God, the relationship between mind and body and scientific method.

But philosophy is also concerned with questions of a very different kind: What should we do? How should we organise society? What is right? How should we understand the idea of justice? On what basis can we choose between different courses of action? These lead to a study of ethics, and of political philosophy and the philosophy of law.

These more immediately practical aspects of philosophy have a long history. Although the pre-socratic philosophers of ancient Greece had probed many questions about the nature of reality, questions to which their answers are still interesting in terms of both epistemology and the natural sciences, with Socrates, as known through Plato, and then Aristotle, the emphasis shifted towards issues of morality. So, for example, Plato's *Republic* is not based on the question 'What is society?' but 'What is justice?', and it is through that question that many other issues about society and how it should be ruled are explored.

Aristotle (in his *Nicomachean Ethics*) asked about the 'good' which was the aim of every action, and about what could constitute a 'final good' – something that was to be sought for its own sake, rather than for the sake of something higher. He came to the view that the highest good for man was *eudaimonia*, which literally means 'having a good spirit', but perhaps can be translated as 'happiness'. He saw it as the state in which a person was fulfilling his or her potential and natural function. It expressed a form of human excellence or virtue (*arete*). This tied in with his general view that everything had a 'final cause': a goal and a purpose to which it moves. If you understand the final cause of something, you also understand its fundamental essence, which finds its expression in that goal. If a knife had a soul, Aristotle argued, that soul would be 'cutting' – that is what makes it a knife, that is what it is there to do. What then is the essence of humankind? What is it there to do? What is its goal?

Aristotle linked his ethics with his whole understanding of human life. He refused to accept any simple rule which could cover all situations, and he also considered human beings in relationship to the society within which they lived, recognising the influence this has on human behaviour. Aristotle saw man as both a 'thinking animal', and also a 'political animal'. It is therefore not surprising that ethics becomes the study of rational choice in action, and that it should have a social as well as an individual aspect. In this chapter we shall take a brief look at some of the main philosophical approaches to moral issues. In the next we shall examine issues of a social and political nature. Although, for convenience, morality and politics are separated, it is important to remember that morality is more than the establishing of a set of personal values. It is equally possible to examine morality in terms of the requirements of the state and the place of individuals within society; the personal and the social cannot be separated in ethics.

'Is' and 'ought'

Once you start to talk about morality, or about the purpose of things, you introduce matters of value as well as those of facts. An important question for philosophy is whether it is possible to derive values from facts, or whether facts must always remain 'neutral'. In other words:

- Facts say what 'is';
- Values say what 'ought' to be;
- Can we ever derive an 'ought' from an 'is'?

If the answer to this question is 'no', then how are we to decide issues of morality? If no facts can be used to establish morality can there be absolute moral rules, or are all moral decisions relative – dependent upon particular circumstances, feelings or desires?

A little later in this chapter we shall examine two ways in which philosophers have presented facts that they consider to be relevant to what people 'ought' to do:

1. An argument based on design and purpose (following Aristotle's comments given above); and
2. An argument based on the expected results of an action.

We shall also examine other features of ethical language: expressing approval or otherwise, recommending a course of action, or expressing emotion. But first, if ethics is to make any sense, we must ask if people are in fact free to decide what to do. If they are not free, if they have no choice, then praise and blame, approval or disapproval are inappropriate. We cannot tell people what they ought to do, unless it is possible for them to do it.

—— Freedom and determinism ——

In the first chapter we saw that, for Kant, space, time and causality were categories used by the human mind to interpret experience. Inevitably, everything in the experienced world is therefore causally conditioned – things don't just happen, they have a reason!

The process of looking for causes, which lies at the heart of the scientific quest, has as its logical goal a totally understood world in which each individual thing and action is explained in terms of all that went before it. In theory, given total knowledge, everything could be predicted. It reflects what we may call the Newtonian world-view, that the universe is like a machine.

We saw that this created problems in terms of the relationship between mind and body. What is the human mind? Can it make a difference? If everything is causally conditioned, then even the electrical impulses in my brain are part of a closed mechanical system. My freedom is an illusion. I may think that I have made a free choice, but in fact everything that has happened to me since my birth, and everything that has made the world the way it is since the beginning of time, has contributed to that decision.

IN OTHER WORDS:

"I just knew you'd say that!" One of the annoying things about people who claim to predict our choices is that we like to think we are free, but are forced to recognise that we may not always be the best judge of ourselves.

One of the fundamental issues of philosophy is freedom and determinism. It is also related to reductionism; that is, the reduction of complex entities (like human beings) to the simpler parts of which they are composed. If we are nothing more than the individual cells that comprise our bodies, and if those cells are determined by physical forces and are predictable, then there seems no room for the whole human being to exercise freedom.

For now, dealing with ethics, one thing is clear:

- If we are free to make a choice, then we can be responsible for what we do. Praise or blame are appropriate. We can act on the basis of values that we hold.
- If we are totally conditioned, we have no choice in what we do, and it makes no sense to speak of moral action springing from choices and values, or action being worthy of praise or blame.

On the other hand, there are levels of determinism. It is clear that nobody is totally free:

1. We have physical limitations. I can't make an unaided leap one hundred feet into the air, even if I feel I have a vocation to do so. Overweight, middle-aged men do not make the best ballet dancers. It's not a matter of choice, merely of physical fact.
2. We may be psychologically predisposed to act in certain ways rather than others. If you are shy and depressed, you are unlikely to be the life and soul of a party. But that is not a matter of choice, merely of present disposition.
3. We may be socially restrained. I may choose to do something really outrageous, but know that I will not get away with it.
4. We may also be limited by the financial and political structures under which we live. There are many things that I cannot do without money, for example.

In considering the moral implications of actions, we have to assess the degree of freedom available to the agent.

Examples:

Is a soldier who is ordered to shoot prisoners or unarmed civilians thereby absolved of moral responsibility? Is he free to choose whether to carry out that act or not? Does the fear of his own death, executed for refusal to obey an order, determine that he must obey?

If a person commits a crime while known to be suffering from a mental illness, or if a psychiatric report indicates that he or she was disturbed at the time, that fact will be taken into account when apportioning blame. But how many people who commit crimes could be described as clear headed and well balanced? How many have no mitigating circumstances of some sort when family background, education, deprivation and other things are considered?

We are all conditioned by many factors; that is not in doubt. The difference between that and determinism, is that determinism leaves no scope for human freedom and choice (we are all automata), whereas those who argue against determinism claim that there remains a measure of freedom that is exercised within the prevailing conditions.

FOR REFLECTION:

Notice how many of the topics studied in philosophy are related to one another. This freedom/determinism issue could be considered in the context of:

- How we understand the world (Kant's idea that we impose causality on all that we experience, so that all phenomena are conditioned);

- The existence of God (Can there be an infinite number of causes? If God knows what I will do, am I free and responsible, or is he?);

- How are scientific laws framed? Can they claim absolute truth? Can we ever be certain that something has caused something else?;

- Is there a self over and above the atoms and cells of which a body is made up? If so, does that self have a life that is independent of the determined life of individual cells?

But keep in mind that moral choice may itself be influenced by our view of the world, of the idea of God, of whether we are totally determined by scientific laws and of whether we have a 'self'. Everything we are, everything we believe, everything we understand about the world is there in the moment when we make a moral choice; not necessarily consciously, but there in the background, exerting an influence.

Not all philosophers have presented the issues of freedom, determinism and moral choice in quite this way. A notable exception in Western thought is Spinoza. He argued that freedom was in fact an illusion, created because we do not know all the causes of our actions. Things that happen to us produce in us either passive or active emotions. The passive emotions, like hatred, anger or fear lead a person into bondage, whereas the active ones are those generated by an understanding of our real circumstances, lead to a positive view of life, and an ability to be ourselves. Spinoza held that the more one understood the world, the more the negative emotions would diminish and be replaced by positive ones. One might perhaps say of this that freedom (and the only freedom that Spinoza will accept) is the ability to see life exactly as it is and say 'Yes' to it.

—— Kinds of ethical language ——

What does it mean to say that something is 'good' or that an action is 'right'? Do these words refer to a hidden quality in that action, something over and above what is actually observed? What sort of evidence can be given for such a description? I can show you what I mean by 'red' by pointing to a range of red objects, and relying on your ability to identify their common feature. Can I do the same by pointing to a range of actions that I consider to be morally right? Take for example:

- A married couple having sexual intercourse.
- Someone helping an blind person across a road.
- Paying for goods in a shop (as opposed to stealing them).

Considering only a description of each action, what have these have in common? Indeed, especially in the case of the sex, there could be a whole range of moral implications which are not included in the physical description. If moral language is not the same as physical description, what is it and how is it justified?

Descriptive ethics

This is the most straightforward form of ethical language. It is simply a description of what happens: what moral choices are made and in which particular circumstances. Rather than making a statement about the rights or wrongs of abortion, for example, descriptive ethics simply gives facts and figures about how many abortions take place, how it is carried out, and what legal restraints there are. **Descriptive ethics is about 'is' rather than 'ought'.**

Normative ethics

Normative ethics deals with the norms of action, in terms of whether an action is considered good or bad, right or wrong. It expresses values, and makes a moral judgement based on them. It may relate to facts, but it is not wholly defined by facts. It may be justified in a number of ways that we shall examine shortly. **Normative ethics is about 'ought'; it makes judgements.**

Meta-ethics

When philosophy examines the claims made in normative ethics, a number of questions are raised.

- What does it mean to say that something is right or wrong?
- Can moral statements be said to be either true or false?
- Do they express more than the preferences of the person who makes them?
- What is the meaning of the terms used in ethical discourse?

These questions are not themselves moral statements; they do not say that any particular thing is right or wrong. Meta-ethics is a branch of philosophy which does to normative ethical statement what philosophy does to language in general. It examines ethical language to find what it means and how it is used.

Meta-ethics produces theories about the nature of ethical language:

Intuitionism

In his book *Principia Ethica* (1903), G E Moore argued that the term 'good' could not be defined, and that every attempt to do so ended in reducing goodness to some other quality which was not common to all 'good' things. In other words, goodness could involve kindness, altruism, generosity, a sense of social justice – but it is not actually defined by any of these. Moore therefore claimed that:

> 'Everyone does in fact understand the question "Is this good?" When he thinks of it, his state of mind is different from what it would be, were he asked "Is this pleasant, or desired, or approved?" It has a distinct meaning for him, even though he may not recognise in what respect it is distinct.'
>
> (*Principia Ethica*, chapter 1)

He likened it to describing the colour yellow. In the end you just have to point to things and say that they are yellow without being able to define the colour. You know what yellow is by intuition. In the same way, you know what goodness is, even though it cannot be defined.

Emotivism

In this theory, saying that something is good or bad is really just a way of expressing what you feel about it. In chapter 1 we saw that, early in the twentieth century, there developed an approach to language known as logical positivism. In this, statements were called meaningless unless they either corresponded to empirical data, or were true by definition. On this basis, moral statements were seen as meaningless. The response to that was to claim that moral statements were not statements about facts, but were performing some other function. Emotivism provides one such function. A moral statement expressed an attitude. It is not true or false by reference to that which it describes, but in respect to its ability to express the emotions of the speaker.

Prescriptivism

This is another response to the challenge of logical positivism. It claims that moral language is actually recommending a course of action. If I say that something is good, I am actually saying that I feel it should be done: in other words, I am recommending it.

Naturalism and metaphysical ethics

G E Moore had argued that you could not get an 'ought' from an 'is' – that you could not derive morality from the facts of human behaviour.

It made a strong distinction between facts and values. On the other hand, from Plato onwards we have seen that some philosophers hold that there are certain principles and values which may be derived from the examination of human beings, their society, and their place within the world as a whole. Naturalism, or metaphysical ethics, is exactly this task.

IN OTHER WORDS:

- If you describe someone's actions or decisions, the truth of what you say is known by checking the facts.

- If you say that something is 'right' or 'wrong', there are no straightforward facts to check in order to verify your claim.

- Meta-ethics therefore looks at these ethical claims and asks what they mean, whether they can be true or false, and, if so, how that truth may be established. If ethics is not about external facts, it may be about intuitions, or emotional responses, or recommendations, or the general structures of life and their implications for individual action.

The theories mentioned above have been developed within the philosophical debate about the nature of language in general and of the status of moral language in particular. But whatever the status of the language they use, the fact is that people do continue to make moral claims. It is therefore important to examine the bases upon which such claims may be made.

——— Three bases for ethics ———

If moral language is simply expressing an emotion or a preference, then it does not seem to need further justification, it implies no more than the feelings of the moment. If we want to argue for a moral position, however, we need to find a rational basis for ethics. Within the history of Western philosophy there have been three principal bases offered – natural law, utilitarianism and the categorical imperative. We shall now examine each of these.

Natural law

From the opening of Aristotle's *Nicomachean Ethics* Book 1:
> 'Every art and every enquiry, and similarly every action and pursuit, is thought to aim at some good; and for this reason the good has rightly been declared to be that at which all things aim.' (1094a)

Aristotle develops this into the idea of the supreme good for human beings: happiness (*eudaimonia*). If you agree with Aristotle that there is a general sense of purpose and a purpose behind everything, a 'good' for which it exists, or if you accept with Plato that the 'forms' (especially the 'Form of the Good') have a permanent reality, independent of our own minds and perceptions, then it would be possible to specify which things are 'good' and which 'bad', which actions are 'right' and which 'wrong' in an independent and objective way.

Natural law claims that something is right if it fulfils its true purpose in life, wrong if it goes against it.

Examples:

Sex Natural law, based on the idea of a natural purpose inherent in everything, might seem particularly appropriate for dealing with issues of sex, since it is clear that sex does have a natural purpose that is essential for life. In natural law terms:

- the 'natural' function of sex is the reproduction of the species;
- non-reproductive sexual activity is 'against nature' and therefore wrong (or at least as a misuse of the natural function of sex). Masturbation, contraception and homosexuality could all be criticised from this standpoint.

Abortion and euthanasia It is natural for every creature to seek and preserve its own life. If everything has a natural purpose to fulfil, then abortion and euthanasia can be seen as wrong, since they go against this natural outworking of the processes of life.

- Unless there is something sufficiently wrong for there to be a miscarriage, the newly fertilised embryo will naturally grow into a new, independent human being. The 'final cause' of the embryo (to use Aristotle's term) is the adult human which it will one day become. It is therefore wrong to frustrate that natural process through abortion.

On a natural law basis, even if the child is not wanted and its life is likely to be an unhappy one, it is still wrong to seek an abortion.

- When the body can no longer sustain the burden of illness, it dies. To anticipate this is to frustrate the natural tendency towards self-preservation. The results of an act of euthanasia may be to lessen a burden of suffering, but it would still be seen as wrong in itself, even if the person making that moral judgement had great sympathy for those involved.

Notice how this approach to ethics relates to the philosophy of religion. The basis of the natural law approach is that the world is purposeful and that the purpose of any part of it may be understood by human reason. It may be seen as the ethical aspect of the traditional argument from design (see p.58).

Natural law is not the same as a consideration of what appears as a natural response to a situation – natural in the sense that it reflects the nature that humankind shares with the rest of the animal kingdom. Rather, it is nature as seen through the eyes of reason; indeed, for most of those who would use a natural law argument, it is also coloured by religious views, with the world seen as the purposeful creation by God.

A newspaper article on adultery was headed 'We have descended from apes but we don't have to behave like them'. In it the author opposed the fashionable theory that is was 'natural' to commit adultery, arguing that although people are instinctively 'bad' they are capable of exercising self-restraint. In particular, she opposed the idea that adultery was simply the natural expression of a genetic urge to reproduce in the most favourable way possible, and that men would therefore 'naturally' be attracted to a number of other women. Part of her argument was put thus:

The near-acceptance of watered-down Freud has allowed juries to accept that murderers were 'temporarily insane'; watered-down Darwin may also soon allow them to accept that rapists were 'temporarily possessed by the genetic need to reproduce'.
But at the heart of all these 'new' explanations for human behaviour lies a fundamental problem: reading about them, it is impossible not to feel that the wheel is being reinvented. To say 'we are all genetic adulterers' is strikingly reminiscent of the similarly strict Christian view of human nature, reflected in the phrase 'we are all sinners'.

... But there is a difference between the world described by neo-Darwinians and the world described by the great religions: the latter believe that the codes and practices which go by the name of morality exist to control our 'natural instincts'.
(Article by Anne Applebaum *The Daily Telegraph* 29 August 1994, p.17)

For reflection:

- Is it possible for something to be natural but wrong?
- Is self-restraint always unnatural?
- Is the genetic strengthening of a species (which presumably could be helped by allowing the strongest to breed freely with the most beautiful) itself a final 'good' to be sought?

IN OTHER WORDS:

- Natural law is not the same thing as the law of nature.

- 'Natural law' is the rational consideration of the final purpose of everything in nature, and the conscious shaping of action to bring it in line with that purpose.

There are many issues within medical ethics that have a 'natural law' component. For example, it is possible to fertilise a human embryo and implant it into the womb of an infertile woman so that she is able to bear a child. Does that mean it is right to do so? In particular, is it right if the woman concerned is beyond normal child-bearing age? (In 1994 a woman aged 59 gave birth to twins, having been given hormones and implanted with embryos by an Italian doctor specialising in such treatment. The case gave rise to considerable medical controversy.)

On the other hand, if such treatment for infertility is branded as 'unnatural', then what are we to say about medicine in general. It may be natural to die from an infection, and unnatural to be saved by an antibiotic. On the other hand, if natural law seeks the fulfilment of each human being, is not the prevention of premature death a decision based on a recognition that an individual might well fulfil his or her potential only after being given a chance to live.

Utilitarianism

Utilitarianism is a moral theory associated particularly with Jeremy Bentham (1748-1832) and J S Mill (1806-73), but its roots are found much earlier.

Hedonism is the term used for a philosophy which makes the achievement of happiness the prime goal in life. Epicurus taught in Athens at the end of the fourth century BCE. He took an atomistic view of the world (everything is composed of indivisible atoms), regarded the gods as having little influence on life, and generally considered the main purpose of life as the gaining of pleasure. Pain, he held, was of shorter duration than pleasure, and death was nothing but the dissolution of the atoms of which we are made, with no afterlife to fear. Wisdom, he argued, should lead to a life free from anxiety, and if morality has any use it is to maximise the amount of pleasure that life can offer.

To be fair to Epicurus, this crude outline does not do justice to the fact that he distinguished the more intellectual pleasures from the animal ones, and that Epicureans were certainly not hedonists in the popular sense. Nevertheless, Epicurus did make the maximising of happiness the prime purpose of morality.

This is the basis of utilitarian theories of ethics. The right thing to do is that which will maximise happiness. It is therefore a theory based on the expected results of an action, rather than any inherent sense of right or wrong. It seeks the maximum happiness for the maximum number of people.

This is very much a common-sense view of ethics; to do what is right is often associated with doing what will benefit the majority. From a philosophical point of view, however, there are certain problems associated with it:

- You can never be certain what the total effects of an action are going to be. To take a crude example, you may save the life of a drowning child who then grows up to be a mass-murderer. In practice, there always has to be a cut-off point beyond which it is not practicable to calculate consequences. Added to this is the fact that we see the result of actions only with hindsight; at the time, we might have expected something quite different. Thus, although utilitarianism seems to offer a straightforward way of assessing moral issues, its assessment must always remain provisional.

- The definition of what constitutes happiness may not be objective. Other people may not want what you deem to be their happiness or best interests. The utilitarian argument appears to make a factual consideration of results the basis of moral choice, but in practice, in selecting the degree or type of happiness to be considered, a person is already making value (and perhaps moral) judgements.

- How do you judge between pain caused to a single individual and the resulting happiness of many others. Would global benefit actually justify the inflicting of pain on a single innocent person?

A silly example:

A perfectly healthy young visitor innocently walks into a hospital in which there are a number of people all waiting for various organ transplants. Might a utilitarian surgeon be tempted?

But a more serious one:

In allocating limited health care budgets, choices have to be made. Do you spend a large amount of money on an operation which may or may not save the life of a seriously ill child if the consequence of that choice is that many other people with debilitating, but perhaps not life-threatening, illnesses are unlikely to receive the help they need?

In Britain in 1994, for example, the cost of neonatal care for babies who were born weighing less than 3 pounds was estimated to be £70 million per year. To add to this, many of these babies were handicapped, and the later cost of caring for them adds £150 million. Of those babies born at 23 weeks, only 10-20 percent survive, and of them half are likely to be severely handicapped.

From a utilitarian position, there are two issues:

1. Is the allocation of limited funds justified, compared with the help that could be given to others?
2. Is the potential suffering of child and parents through severe handicap such that survival does not add to the total sum of happiness?

Further difficulties arise in a consideration of the second of these examples, in that experimental surgical procedures carried out today may benefit many more patients in the more distant future. The argument for fundamental research in the sciences is often justified on this basis – that without it, the long-term development of new technology will be stifled.

Forms of utilitarianism

So far we have considered only **act utilitarianism**. This makes moral judgements on the basis of the likely consequences of particular acts. There is also **rule utilitarianism**, which considers the overall benefit that will be gained by society if a particular rule is accepted. In other words, breaking a rule may benefit the individual concerned, but allowing that rule to be broken whenever an individual may benefit may itself have harmful consequences to society as a whole. This was a form of utilitarianism put forward by J S Mill. There are two forms of rule utilitarianism: strong and weak. A strong rule utilitarian will argue that it is never right to break a rule if that rule is to the benefit of society as a whole. A weak rule utilitarian will argue that there may be special cases in which breaking the rule is allowed, although the overall benefit to society of not doing so should also be taken into consideration. Preference utilitarianism is based on taking the preferences of all those who are involved into account. (In other words, the basis on which the 'good' is assessed is not impersonal, but is as perceived in that particular situation.)

A situation:

In October 1994 the British government launched a campaign to vaccinate all children against rubella. This caused problems for Catholics, since the rubella vaccine was originally developed from a dead foetus. The ethical arguments show the clash between 'natural law' and utilitarian concerns. At first, two Catholic schools opted out of vaccination on grounds that:
> 'absolute respect for human life requires the condemnation of direct abortion and a refusal to benefit from the products of an evil action.'

In other words, if the original abortion was wrong in itself, then no amount of good coming from it subsequently can make it right. If a person knowingly benefits from something that is wrong, he or she appears to condone it.

The Catholic Bishops then gave parents a free choice, allowing

---

that some would want to take a prophetic stand against abortion, but adding that 'Catholic parents who wish to consent to its use can be assured that there is no general obligation to refuse permission ... Consenting does not condone abortion nor amount to encouraging further abortions for this vaccine.'

In other words, if you benefit from a result of an action, that does not in itself imply that you approve of it.

A spokesman for one of the schools which refused the vaccine to boys, nevertheless accepted that it could be given to girls, because of the danger that rubella during pregnancy can damage the unborn child.

Here the form of argument seems to have switched to a utilitarian one. In fact, it is possible to argue that the refusal to accept the vaccine could also be justified on utilitarian grounds if it is believed that, as a rule, the opposition to abortion will produce greater benefits than the avoidance of rubella.

This example illustrates the fact that, although for the purpose of ethics we tend to separate off the different forms of argument, when dealing with actual moral issues both arguments may be used, and the moral judgement is a matter of balancing their competing claims. There is seldom a straight choice, and wishing to avoid rubella is not the same thing as approving of abortion.

Both utilitarianism and natural law appear to give rational and objective bases for deciding between right and wrong. Both of them, however, have presuppositions which are not accounted for by the theory itself. The one depends on the idea of a rational final cause, the other on the acceptance of happiness as the highest good.

The categorical imperative

The third of our bases for ethical decisions comes from Kant. In the first chapter we saw the way in which Kant made a radical distinction between things as we perceive them and things as they are in themselves. The latter, he argued, were unknowable. The former were known through the categories by which the human mind understands all experience – categories which include space, time and causality.

Kant also argued that, in order to act morally, a person would actually have three presuppositions: God, freedom and immortality.

- Freedom is, as we have already seen, necessary if there are to be moral choices. For Kant, a person is noumenally free (i.e. free in himself or herself) but phenomenally conditioned (i.e. from the standpoint of an observer, all actions would have causes).
- God was also necessary, for otherwise there would be no guarantee that doing what was right would lead ultimately to the highest good (this being guaranteed by God).
- But even if doing the right thing were to lead to the highest good, this might not be possible within the span of a single human life (e.g. if someone gives his or her life to save another), therefore we must assume some form of immortality.

Notice that Kant did not think that a person would first come to a rational acceptance of God, freedom and immortality and then decide to be moral. Rather, by acting morally, even by feeling a sense of moral obligation, a person (consciously or unconsciously) displays a belief in these three things.

The sense of moral obligation is termed the **categorical imperative**, since is 'categorical' (i.e. absolute, rather than based on particular circumstances or expected results). Whereas a utilitarian basis for action depended on predicting results of particular actions, the categorical imperative is general – applying to all situations.

Kant expressed the categorical imperative in various ways, but it amounts to this:
Act only on that maxim (or principle) which you can – at the same time – will that it should become a universal law.

and to this he added a second principle:
Act is such a way as to treat people as ends and never as means.

The first of these amount to the principle that whatever one wishes to do, one should be prepared for everyone else to do it as well. If you cannot wish that you action become a universal rule, then you should not do it in your individual circumstances.

Here you have the most general of all principles, and one which, on the surface, has a long pedigree. It follows from the golden rule – to do to others only that which you would wish them to do to you.

One problem with this is that there may be circumstances in which a person may want to kill or lie, without wishing for killing or lying to become universal. Suppose, for example, that the life of an innocent person is being threatened, and the only way of saving him or her is by lying, then a person would wish to do so. In this case, following Kant's argument, one would need to argue that you could wish that anyone in an identical situation should be free to lie, without thereby willing that anyone in any situation should be free to do so. Kant himself recognised the problem with this particular situation – his own example being of the person in need who borrows money promising to repay it, but knowing that he is unable to do so.

IN OTHER WORDS:

Natural law, the assessment of results, and the sense of moral obligation: these three (sometimes singly, sometimes mixed together) form the basis of much moral argument. They usually lead to general moral principles – that this or that sort of action is right or wrong. It is quite another matter whether it is fair to apply any such general rule to each and every situation.

The absolute v. the relative in morality

If morality is absolute, then a particular action may be considered wrong no matter what the circumstances. So, for example, theft may be considered to be wrong. But what is theft? In one sense the definition is straightforward: theft is the action of taking what belongs to another without that person's consent. The problem is that 'theft' is a term that may be used to interpret individual situations. Can we always be sure that it is the right term? If not, then is it right to treat an action as morally equal to 'theft', if that is not the way one or more of the people concerned see the matter.

One example of this dilemma might be 'mercy killing', where someone who is seriously ill and facing the prospect of a painful or lingering death is helped to die by a relative or close friend. If you take a view that there are moral absolutes, you may say 'Murder is always wrong.' The next question then becomes, 'Is mercy killing the same thing as murder?' In other words, you start with absolute moral principles and then assess each particular situation in terms of which of these moral principles are involved (a process that is generally termed 'casuistry').

If you do not think that there are moral absolutes, you are more likely to start with particular situations and assess the particular intentions and consequences involved. In making such an assessment you bring to bear your general views about life and of the implications that various actions have on society as a whole. Even the ethical arguments (e.g. 'situation ethics') which deny the validity of general rules, cannot assess any situation in a vacuum.

To illustrate the complexities of applying general rules of particular situations, let us take one actual example of what is generally known as 'date rape'. This is the term used when a charge of rape is made against a person known to the 'victim' and carried out in the course of a date. Date rape is a good example of the ambiguities that arise in legal and moral debates, since any straightforward description of the situation (sexual intercourse against the will of one partner – or, in the particular case we shall be examining, attempted intercourse) is made more complicated by the circumstances in which it takes place, namely that the two people involved have chosen to be together socially.

In December 1992, a solicitor took a colleague to a ball at a London hotel. Each had assumptions about the nature of the relationship between them that was established by his inviting her to the ball and her accepting that invitation. She made a complaint against him, and he was charged with attempted rape. According to a newspaper report:

The court had been told he committed the offence after a night of dancing reels and drinking whisky and champagne with his victim, known throughout the trial as Miss X. She invited him to share a room at a friend's ... flat, but said she awoke to find him on top of her, wearing only his frilly cuffs and a green condom.

A comment, based on the original trial details, added:

There were those who argued passionately that Miss X, by undressing down to her knickers in full view of him, at worst was sending out sexual signals, and at best was behaving foolishly and should shoulder some responsibility for what followed.

[*Daily Telegraph* 1 October 1994, p.5]

At the trial, he was found guilty of attempted rape and sentenced to three years in prison. This was later reduced to two years on appeal. He was released after serving half this sentence, on grounds of good conduct, but (at the time of his release) it was anticipated that he would face a disciplinary hearing before the Solicitors' Complaints Bureau, with a good chance that he would be prevented from continuing with his legal career.

Matters to be taken into consideration in the defence of a person charged with attempted rape in these circumstances:

- If one person invites another to share a room, is that invitation to be taken as at least implying that the idea of having some sort of sexual relationship is not out of the question. (i.e. the invitation to share a room might not be a direct invitation to have sex, but might it not suggest that the matter is at least a possibility).

- Does an act of sexual intercourse between two people who have voluntarily shared some time together (i.e. on a 'date') require a specific act of verbal consent?

- If no specific verbal or written consent is given (i.e. there is no exchange of contracts before clothes are removed – even between solicitors!) does a mis-interpretation of the situation by one party constitute rape or attempted rape?

- Consider another possibility. If a woman were to invite a man back to her room after such an evening, hoping for sex (and under the impression that he was willing), but the man – perhaps because of a excess of whisky – were to fall asleep on the sofa, could she take a civil action against him for breach of implied promise?

- In such circumstances, is the action 'rape' or simply misunderstanding?

- Can the act of undressing before another person be considered 'contributory negligence' if a rape or attempted rape ensues?

On the other hand, a person bringing the charge of date rape could argue:

- That rape, violence and other forms of abuse often take place between people who know one another. The fact of their previous relationship does not lessen the seriousness of the action that takes place, or that is threatened.

- That there can be no objective proof of misunderstanding. Claiming that you misunderstood something may be a later rationale of the situation, or an excuse.

The problem for ethics is that a unique situation may be understood in many different ways. The words chosen (e.g. attempted rape) interpret, rather than describe, the event. Even if it were agreed that rape is always morally wrong, there remains the problem of deciding exactly when that term should be used. Hence there may need to be flexibility, even within a framework of absolute moral values.

On the other hand, allowing each event to determine its own rules is likely to lead to moral and social chaos. One approach to ethics which emphasises the uniqueness of events is **situation ethics**. This argues that rules do not do justice to the uniqueness of individual situations, and that it is best to interpret each in the light of general principles – like 'Do whatever is the most loving thing.' This attempts to balance freedom with the need for certain basic concepts (e.g. love) to guide action.

So far we have been mainly been looking at situations of individual moral choice. But there is another dimension to ethics: the social.

—————— Values and society ——————

The sort of moral choices that a person makes are based on the values that he or she holds. Those who wish to foster a sense of moral responsibility within society as a whole are likely to be concerned to promote values that command wide acceptance. If those values are accepted, then appropriate patterns of behaviour can be expected to follow from them:

Here is a list of such values, given by a British politician, the former Education Secretary, John Patten:
Self-reliance and self-discipline; acceptance of responsibility; regard for proper authority; unselfishness and the need for self-restraint; dignity, courtesy and respect for others; honesty and trustworthiness; and last but not least, loyalty and fidelity.

All of these are vital and used to be common ground; alas moral relativism, that particularly nasty and new late-twentieth century ingredient, has caused so many of our own moral problems. 'Anything goes', 'there's always an excuse', and all the rest of the politically correct received ideas have wrought havoc.
[*Daily Telegraph* 21 September 1994, p.25]

Few would disagree that the values he lists are worthwhile, and lead to a heightened moral and social awareness. The dilemma concerns what he means by relativism in this context. Relativism can mean:

1. That there are no fixed rules that determine how a particular set of values shall be translated into actions; or
2. That within a particular society or era there are different sets of values, which therefore give rise to different moral codes.

What John Patten seems to be saying here is that many people in society lack values of their own, and have scant regard for those of others. 'Anything goes' implies no shared values.

But 'there's always an excuse' is rather different. This suggests that actions are determined (by upbringing, by circumstances, by psychological or sociological conditioning), rather than free and responsible. But there is a further implication, which is that actions are determined by the impact on the individual of the attitudes and values of society as a whole. Moral responsibility is therefore seen as shifted back from the individual to society. 'Received ideas' are to blame. Although moral choices are made by individuals, the environment within which they make those decisions, and the attempts they make to justify them, are coloured by political and economic conditioning.

We therefore need to examine the philosophy of politics, for, whether we are determined or free, our values and actions will be influenced (to say the least) by our society – and that is a fact that philosophers since Plato have been quick to recognise.

IN OTHER WORDS:

- Ethics is the study of morality and of moral language.
- Moral values may be based on: a view of the world in which everything is designed for a purpose (natural law); the expected results of an action (utilitarianism); a sense of absolute moral obligation (the categorical imperative).
- General moral principles have to be balanced against the uniqueness of particular situations.
- The actions of individuals need to be examined in terms of the general attitudes and values of the society within which they live.

[Ethics is a huge subject, both in terms of its philosophical basis and the range of modern moral issues which can be explored. For further treatment of some of these issues see *Teach Yourself: Ethics.*]

6

PHILOSOPHY AND POLITICS

In 1993, the British Prime Minister, John Major, used the phrase 'Back to basics' to provide a focus for his political stance. But what exactly did it mean?

- Did it mean back to the basis or bases of the political system? If so what are they? (John Major himself started to develop this approach, in response to the debate over 'back to basics', speaking of the importance of the freedom of the individual.)
- Some people gained the impression that it meant 'back to basic values'. So, for example, if a politician is caught in an embarrassing sexual situation, that might be thought to go against basic values. And behind that lies the more general question about whether family values should be seen as basic.
- But are you talking about basic human needs, feelings and natural urges? If so, the poor politician caught with his trousers down is as near to such basics as you can get!
- What is the 'basis' of civilised life?
- What basic values can be agreed on? Can we agree on any? Is a basis something you start from and then develop, or is it something fixed and unchanging to which you have to return, tail between your legs, from time to time.

Starting with the phrase 'back to basics', we have entered into some of the issues with which political philosophy is concerned. Set out in more abstract terms these concerns are:

- the concepts of freedom, justice, liberty and equality;
- the role of the state;
- the relationship between the state and the individual;
- the nature of authority;

- the status of law;
- the role of power;
- human rights.

——————— **Only individuals?** ———————

Does the state exist? Is there any such thing as society? If I were suddenly to declare that the United States did not exist, I would be thought insane, but is it that obvious? There are two ways of looking at individuals and society:

1. Society, or the nation, is a reality over and above its individual citizens. It is 'real' in the sense that it can exert its power over them, forcing them to take part in a war, claiming taxes from them, imposing laws on them. Patriotism depends on having an idea of this reality.
2. There is no such thing as society. There are just individuals who cooperate, who decide on rules and regulations for their mutual benefit, who band together to do things that are beyond the abilities of any one individual or family. In this case, 'Great Britain' is just a name: the name given to those millions of people who live in that part of the world, and to the various institutions by which they organise their lives.

If you tend towards the first of these, you might take a further step and claim that individuals can only exist as part of larger social groups. You could argue, for example:

- that you are part of a family and circle of friends: you are a mother, father, child or friend by virtue of your relationships. Without other people you would be none of these things.
- that you speak a language that is not of your own devising. You share in a common store of words and thoughts. Without society, there would be no language. You have 'rights' as an individual only because they are given to you by society.

Therefore, although you would continue to be a human being, you would not really be an 'individual', with a name, rights, a language and a stock of inherited ideas, without society.

IN OTHER WORDS:

Confronted by a cat, a mouse cannot argue its case for the right to life, liberty and happiness. Individual rights or social obligations are not discovered in nature, they are devised by society. Without society there would be no rights, no obligations, no laws, no morality.

The idea of the individual or citizen is closely linked to that of society or the state. Each is defined with reference to the other. A central issue for the philosophy of politics is to find an acceptable balance between these two things. Individualism; democracy; totalitarianism; socialism; cultural imperialism; regionalism; internationalism: these are all about the balance between individuals or groups and the larger social wholes of which they are a part.

Examples:

- Within the European Union, do you look to the overall benefit of a unified political and monetary system, or do you emphasise the needs of (or threat to) local decision making by individual states?
- Is the United Nations the emerging global 'state' of the future, within which individual nations need to subsume their own interests for the sake of a greater good? Or is it simply a group of individual nations banded together for mutual protection and benefit, within which each will seek to gain as much for itself as is compatible with retaining membership?
- What does it mean to be a good member of a team or a company?

The social contract

Self-preservation is a fundamental human need. Born in 1588, **Thomas Hobbes** knew first hand the traumas of civil war in England and used such a lawless and dangerous state as the starting point for his political theory. In chapter 13 of *Leviathan*, published in 1651, he considers what life is like when a person can rely only on his own strength for protection:

In such condition, there is no place for industry, because the fruit thereof is uncertain; and consequently no culture of the earth; no navigation, nor use of the commodities that may be imported by sea; no commodious building, no instruments of moving or removing such things as require much force; no knowledge of the face of the earth; no account of time; no arts; no letters; no society; and, which is worst of all, continual fear and danger of violent death; and the life of man solitary, poor, nasty, brutish, and short.

Hobbes considered that the need for self-preservation was so basic to human life, that (using a 'natural law' form or argument) reason could show that the basis for political science was the preservation of the life. He also showed, in the passage quoted above, that society depends upon personal security, and that without it civilisation is impossible. The value of the state is seen in its ability to protect and benefit the individuals of which it is comprised.

In this situation, Hobbes argued that people would band together for their mutual protection, and would set up a ruler who would maintain order. His political theory, the start of what is called the 'social contract' tradition, springs from this need for self preservation. Hobbes believed, however, that the ruler so appointed should be given absolute power, and that only by doing so could the security of the state be maintained.

John Locke (1632-1704) argued from a similar starting point. He saw the laws imposed by a ruler on individuals as based on the need for the preservation of life and private property within the state, and defence from foreign threats. But he went beyond Hobbes, in that he argued that the people who entered into their social contract should have the right, if the rulers did not benefit them, to replace them with others. In other words, he argued for a representative democracy, with rulers accountable to those who have put them in power. Thus we have a constitutional government, where rulers have power, but only to the extent that they are given it by the people, and within principles that are set out within a constitution.

IN OTHER WORDS:

For Hobbes and Locke, the moral justification for the actions of the state is utilitarian (see chapter 5), a view taken by Bentham and Mill (see his essays *On Liberty* and *On Representative Government*). Government is by the people and for the benefit of the people.

Such political systems are based on a social contract: on the agreement between people that they shall act together for their mutual benefit. The problem arises over exactly what is to the benefit of society, and who is to decide it. To what extent can an individual, on the basis of a social contract, act on behalf of all? Do all have to agree before some action is taken? On what basis is there to be arbitration between conflicting interests. Locke is clear that decisions must reflect the wishes of a majority, and any minority must accept that judgement:

> ... every man, by consenting with others to make one body politic under one government, puts himself under an obligation to every one of that society to submit to the determination of the majority, and to be concluded by it; or else this original compact, whereby he with others incorporates into one society, would signify nothing, and be no compact if he be left free and under no other ties than he was in before in the state of Nature.
>
> [*The Second Treatise of Government*, chapter 13, section 97]

Thus a government can act as long as it has the consent of a majority. But what if a government seeks to act in a way which the rulers consider to be in the interests of the people, even if that is not what people as individuals actually want?

Questions to consider:
- When is it right to disobey the law?
- Is civil disobedience justified in a democracy?
- Does its support by a majority of people itself justify the actions carried out by a democratic government?

The general will

Jean-Jacques Rousseau (1712-78), recognising that all existing states were imperfect, sought to start from first principles and establish the basis of a legitimate political system. Like Hobbes and Locke, he looked back to man in a state of nature but, unlike them, he thought that in such a natural state people's needs would be few and relatively easily satisfied, and would be unlikely to lead to conflict.

By contrast, once society becomes established, people enclose property and deprive others of the use of it. The basic requirements of food and shelter become commodities which people have to get through barter, and many are therefore reduced to misery. With private property, inequality increases and leads to civil strife. Thus, where Hobbes and Locke saw private property as a natural right to be defended, Rousseau saw it as something artificially imposed by society. In this way, society tends to corrupt natural man rather than improve him.

Rousseau presents a form of social contract, but this differs significantly from that set out by Hobbes or Locke. A central issue of Rousseau is how an individual can retain his or her freedom, whilst at the same time accepting the terms of a social contract, and the requirement that an individual is bound by the wishes of society as a whole. He does this through the idea of the 'general will'. He argues that an individual must give himself or herself totally, including all his rights, to the whole community. The 'general will' is sovereign, and individuals find their own freedom by conforming to it.

For Rousseau, natural freedom is in fact a slavery to individual passions. By contrast, to set aside one's individual, personal will, and to accept the general will, is to discover one's higher aspirations and moral freedom. There will be occasions when an individual will go against the general will, but on those occasions the individual concerned may accept (or be forced to accept) the general will.

Of course, in any political system there will be general laws and also the application of them to individual situations. Now, if everyone is to accept the general will, then it cannot be concerned with indivudual disputes – for those are exactly situations in which individuals disagree. Because of this there has to be a legislator, who will recommend and apply laws, but will do so only with the consent of the general will.

In general, one might say that, whereas for Hobbes and Locke individuals are freely able to decide what is in their own best interests (although sometimes required to set these interests aside for the benefit of the majority), for Rousseau, individuals are not able to decide what is best, and therefore are required to accept what is deemed to be best by the general will – in other words, by the state.

This line of thinking, in which the state acts for the good of all, and in which people act and find their freedom within a political process rather than as independent individuals, leads us to look very briefly at Marxist political philosophy.

Karl Marx (1818-83) argued that religion, morality, political ideas and social structures were fundamentally rooted in economics – particularly the production and distribution of goods. People have basic needs which must be fulfilled in order for them to live, and society becomes more and more sophisticated in order to produce the goods and services to meet those needs. He therefore interpreted history in economic terms. He saw history as shaped by the struggle between different social classes. The bourgeois confront the proletariat; employers facing employees as once landowners faced their peasants. Individual actions are judged by the way in which they contribute to the class struggle, and the actions of a class as a whole is seen in a broader context of the movement of society.

In terms of the history of philosophy, Marx was influenced by Hegel. Like Hegel, he saw reality as working itself out through a process of change. Hegel had introduced the idea of a 'dialectic': first you have a thesis, then in response to this you have the opposite (an 'antithesis'), and bringing these two together you get a 'synthesis'. But for Hegel, this process was mental; the mind develops through this dialectic. For Marx, by contrast, the process of dialectic is material. It is the economic conditions under which the classes live and work that produces the urge to change, as a result of which the existing economic system is overthrown through a revolution and a new system is set up, but that, in turn, leads to further class confrontation, and so on. Marx looked towards the achievement of a classless society, where there would be no more confrontation, but where working people would own the means of production and distribution. This classless society would therefore be characterised by economic justice, in which each benefitted from his or her own labour.

This was linked to his view of the fulfilment of the human individual. Marx argued that, in a capitalist system, an individual who works for a wage, producing something from which someone else is going to make a profit, becomes alienated from that working situation. He or she cannot exercise true creativity or humanity, but becomes an impersonal 'thing', a machine whose sole purpose in life is production, a means of making 'capital'. He saw this process leading to more and more wealth being concentrated in the hands of a small number of 'bourgeosie', with the working proletariat sinking into poverty. This, he believed, would eventually lead to the overthrow of the capitalist system by the workers acting together. He believed that, with the classless society, each individual would be able to develop to his or her full potential.

Marxist philosophy has been extremely influential. It has things to say about the nature of history, of work, of the self, of political institutions, of social classes. He is also a prime example of the way in which a philosopher can influence the course of history. It is difficult to study Marx without being aware of the global impact of Marxist ideology in the twentieth century. The decline of communism in the last decades of the twentieth century, and capitalism's failure to self-destruct in the way he predicted, will obviously be taken into account by anyone who studies his political philosophy. On the other hand, it is difficult to overestimate the general impact of his thinking, particularly perhaps in the view that politics is based on economics. Although Marx' main work was *Das Kapital* (1867), it may be easier to approach him through the earlier works, particularly *The German Ideology* (1846) and *The Communist Manifesto* (1848).

Notice that Marx (following Rousseau and also Hegel) saw the individual as subsuming his or her interests for the benefit of the wider group. The individual acts as a representative of his or her class or nation, and those actions are judged by whatever is deemed to be right by that larger social group. This is in contrast to the tradition which stems from Hobbes and Locke, where the emphasis is on the individual. We shall see in the next section that this divide is still found in political philosophy, as reflected in the differing views of justice taken by two modern philosophers, Rawls and Nozick.

IN OTHER WORDS:

In looking at political theory, it is possible to take the individual or society as a whole as the starting point. From the individual point of view, there are theories of social contract, by which free individuals come together for mutual benefit (Hobbes; Locke). On the other hand, if the social group takes precedence, the individual is required to find his or her freedom in accepting and working within the general will (Rousseau; Marx).

Justice

The idea of justice is fundamental to political philosophy. If people are to band together for mutual protection, if they are to enter into social contracts, if they are to set their own interests aside, they need to be persuaded that the society within which they live is based on principles that are just. But what constitutes political justice?

We shall look at ideas of justice presented by three philosophers, one ancient and two modern:

Plato

The question 'What is justice?' dominates one of the greatest works of philosophy, Plato's *The Republic*. In this dialogue, Plato has Socrates reject the idea that justice is a matter of acting in the interests of the stronger – in other words, that those with power decide what is right, and others follow that out of fear. On the other hand, all that is needed is to appear to be just, not to actually be just. Glaucon (one of the protagonists) therefore introduces the story of Gyges ring. This ring enables its wearer to become invisible at will, and therefore to escape any consequences of his or her actions. If one's actions do not have consequences, why should one be just? What is the value of justice in itself?

Socrates considers the various classes of people that make up the city, and argues that each class offers particular virtues, but that justice is found in the fact that each class performs its own task. In the same way, the individual soul is divided into three parts – mind, spirit and appetite – and that justice for the individual consists in the balance, with each part performing its own task for the benefit of that individual.

Justice is seen in the harmony and proper functioning of each part of society, and Plato wanted the rulers of his Republic to be philosophers, seeking only the truth and not following their base instincts. This, he argued, would be necessary if justice was to be established for all, rather than in the interests of a particular section of the population.

Every philosophy needs to be seen against the background of its particular time and society, and Plato is no exception. His concept of a state ruled by philosophers, seeking a balance between elements in society and in the self, with priority given to the intellectual faculty, is not easily translated into a modern context. It is clear, however, that Plato did not see justice as equality, nor in sectional interest (he rejected the idea that it was the interest of the stronger), but in a balance in which different people and classes, each doing what is appropriate for them, work together for the common good.

Rawls (justice as fairness)

In his work *A Theory of Justice* (1972) John Rawls starts with the idea of a group of people who come together to decide the principles upon which their political association should operate. In other words, they set about forming a social contract. But he adds one further important thing: that they should forget everything about themselves as individuals. They do not know if they are poor or wealthy, men or women. They do not know their race or their position within society. They come together simply as individuals, nothing more. He therefore seeks by this means to establish principles that

> 'free and rational persons concerned to further their own interests would accept in an initial position of equality as defining the fundamental terms of their association.' (p.11)

In other words, they are concerned to benefit themselves, but do not know who they are. By this means, Rawls hopes to achieve justice, for each person will want to legislate for the benefit of themselves, whoever they eventually turn out to be.

Rawls argues that such a group would require two principles:

1. Liberty. Each person should have equal rights to as extensive a set of basic liberties as possible, as long as that does not prevent others from having a similar set of fundamental liberties.
2. Distribution of resources. Given that there are social inequalities, Rawls argues that the distribution of resources should be such that the least advantaged in society receive the greatest benefit.

This is justice based on 'fairness'. Rawls argues that it is fair to grant everyone equal freedom and opportunity, and that, if there is to be inequality at all, it should only be allowed on the grounds that it benefits those who have the least advantages in life. The task of society (in addition to the basic protection of individuals who have come together to form it) is, according to Rawls, that it should organise the fair sharing out of both material and social benefits.

Not all philosophers would agree with Rawls' attempt to reduce inequalities. In the last century, Nietzsche's view was that the strong should not be restrained because of the needs of the weak. His views were that democracy and Christianity had a negative effect, weakening the human species by seeking special advantage for those who are weak or poor and handicapped in some way. By contrast, he looked towards an *Ubermensch* – an 'over-man' or 'beyond-man', expressing the idea of striving to be something more. For Nietzsche, man is something that has to be overcome: a starting point from which we move forward and upward.

But there is a more general criticism of his approach. A little earlier in this chapter we looked at the basic division between those who would give priority to the individual (for whom the state should have a minimal role, and who may go so far as to argue that the state does not exist), and those who give priority to the state, so that it is only in the context of society that individuals come to their full potential. Let us examine Rawls' theory from this perspective.

By making the people who come together to establish the principles of society forget who they are, they also relinquish all that they might naturally have gained and achieved. The successful person is made to forget all that he or she has gained by hard work, and to opt for an equal share of the pooled resources for fear of finding out that he or she was, in fact, the poorest.

This theory does establish a society which (by seeing all people as equal) offers fair shares. But are real people in an actual society like that? It can be argued that there never was, and never will be, an original position from which to start the process of making the rules of a society, all actual legal systems, and all ideas of justice are framed within an historical context.

Another criticism of this approach is made by Ronald Dworkin. He argues that, before you can ask 'What is justice?' you need to ask the prior question 'What kind of life should men and women lead? What counts as excellence in a human being?' He argues that the liberal position, as given by Rawls, does not take this into consideration. The treatment of individuals does not depend on anything about them as individuals.

For reflection:

If every inequality is allowed only on the basis that it benefits the least well off (Rawls' view), there is little chance that excellence will be developed, since every facility offered for the development of excellence is likely to increase rather than decrease the gap between the most able and the least able. How can such a theory avoid bland mediocrity?

Nozick (justice as entitlement)

If the purpose of society is to protect the life, liberty and property of individuals, then each person should be enabled to retain those things which are rightly his or hers. A society which, in the name of establishing equality, redistributes that wealth is in fact depriving an individual of the very protection which led to the formation of society in the first place.

This approach to the question of justice is taken by Robert Nozick. In *Anarchy, State and Utopia* (1974), he argued that it is wrong for the state to take taxes from individuals or force them to contribute to a health service that benefits others. It infringes their liberty to gain wealth and retain it. For Nozick, it is perfectly right to give what you have to another person if you so choose, but not to demand that another person give to you. On this social theory, voluntary contributions are welcomed, but enforced taxes are not. He argues that justice is a matter of the entitlement of individuals to retain their 'holdings', wealth that they have gained legitimately.

An important feature of Nozick's case is that, at any one time, the actual wealth that a person owns is related to history: that of the individual (through having worked for years, for example) or that of his or her family (through inheritance). In practice, however, it is not always easy to establish that all wealth has been gained legitimately. Land which has been in a family for generations may originally have been gained by the most dubious of means.

Nozick also argues, against those that seek equality, that even if people were made equal, they would immediately start trading, and would quickly establish new inequalities.

IN OTHER WORDS:

- Private property is theft (which implied that all property should belong to the state, or ultimately to the global community)! Justice demands redistribution on the basis of need;

OR

- Redistribution is theft (which implies that each individual has the right to that which is lawfully gained)! Justice demands that each should develop to his or her potential, unhampered by false notions of equality.

—— Individual freedom and the law ——

Freedom in this context means something rather different from the 'freedom/determinism' debate outlined earlier. In that case, the determinist argues that we are never free to choose what we do, but that everything can be determined. Here, the debate is about the degree of freedom that the individual has a right to exercise within society, given the impact that such freedom may have upon the freedom of others: freedom to act within certain parameters set out by the law. Once a person acts outside those parameters, society, through the police and the courts, can step in and impose a penalty on the 'outlaw'.

Taking a utilitarian view of morality (see chapter 5), J S Mill argued that in the case of some private matter, where an action and its consequences affect only the individual concerned, there should be absolute freedom. The law should step in to restrain that freedom only when the consequences of an action affected other people. This is the common-sense basis for much legislation.

An example:

If smoking cigarettes were a private activity, with consequences, however harmful, suffered only by the person who chooses to smoke, there would be no need to legislate against it. The law may step in to prohibit smoking in public places if 1) it constitutes a fire hazard, or 2) non-smokers want to be free to breathe air that is not filled with smoke.

Legislation can be justified on a simple, utilitarian basis. The law protects other people from the effects of an individual's action.

But should society as a whole, through its medical services, be required to pay the price for an individual's decision to smoke, take drugs, or practise a dangerous sport? Here the law has to balance a utilitarian moral position with the preservation of individual human rights.

The idea of individual liberty has been of fundamental importance in modern political thinking, responding perhaps to the experience of horrific excesses of twentieth century totalitarian systems, in Nazi Germany, the Soviet Union and elsewhere. Karl Popper's book *The*

Open Society and its Enemies, published in the 1940s, made the issue of freedom central. In the 1960s, much political debate centred on how to maintain social order and yet allow maximum freedom. Rawls' theory of justice may be seen as an attempt to justify liberal views of society, and in which the redistribution of wealth is a logical choice of free individuals. Rawls took the view that, provided all the essentials of life were met (a presupposition of his theory), people would choose freedom, rather than, for example, the chance of getting more wealth. This view has been challenged by Ronald Dworkin and others, who think that some people would rather gamble that they would win, rather than play it safe and follow the liberal and egalitarian views of Rawls.

Human rights

The law is framed on the basis of the agreement of free individuals, and every person is seen as having basic human rights. On the other hand, there is a difference between having a set of rights, and being free to exercise those rights. In general, even though rights are given irrespective of age and capacities, it is sometimes necessary for the exercise of those rights to be curtailed:

• on grounds of age. Children have rights, and are protected by the law from exploitation by others, but cannot, for example, buy cigarettes or alcohol, drive a car or fly a plane. These limits are imposed because below the relevant age the child is not considered to be able to take a responsible decision and parents, or society, therefore impose a restriction on the child's freedom;
• on grounds of insanity. Those who are insane and are liable to be a danger to themselves or to others are also restrained;
• on grounds of lack of skill. Flying a plane or driving a car (other than on private property) without a licence is illegal. This can be justified on utilitarian grounds, since others in the air or on the roads could be in danger. Equally, to pose as a surgeon and perform operations without qualifications is illegal. Without public acceptance of the required skills, many such tasks would endanger the lives or well-being of others.

Rights are also taken from those who break the law, for example:

• through prison sentences;
• through legal injunctions to stop actions being carried out or to

prevent one person from approaching another, or visiting a particular place. This may be taken retrospectively, if a person has already broken a law, or proactively, for example, to stop publication of a potentially damaging story in a newspaper.

In all these cases, a person retains his or her fundamental rights, but cannot exercise them, on the basis that to do so would be against the interests of society as a whole. This approach is based on the idea of social contract, where the laws of society are made by mutual agreement, and the loss of certain freedoms are exchanged for the gain of a measure of social protection. It may also therefore be justified on utilitarian grounds.

But Dworkin argues that a 'right' is something that an individual can exercise even if it goes against the general welfare. After all, there is no point in my claiming a right to do something, if nobody would ever want to challenge it. A right is something that I can claim in difficult circumstances.

This means that (at least in the immediate context) rights cannot be justified on utilitarian grounds. They do not necessarily offer the greatest good to the greatest number. Rights are claimed by minorities. Rights are established by social contract (e.g. within the American constitution) and represent a basic standard of treatment that people can expect to receive.

IN OTHER WORDS:

- Individual freedom needs to be balanced against the needs of society as a whole. The morality of exercising individual freedom may be assesed on utilitarian grounds.
- Human rights represent the basic freedoms and opportunities that an individual can expect to receive from society. They may sometimes be withheld if their exercise would pose a threat to the individual or society as a whole.
- The exercise of human rights cannot always be justified on utilitarian grounds. It is important for an individual to be able to claim a right, even if it is not to the benefit of the majority.

—————— Some conclusions ——————

The problem with political philosophy (and perhaps with all philosophy) is that it works with abstract and generalised concepts, and seldom does justice to the actual situation within which people find themselves. The world is complex. Wealth in one place is gained at the expense of poverty in another. A 'free' market will lead some to success, others to failure. Laws that benefit those who want to retain their wealth are seen by those who are the least privileged as an excuse for continued greed.

What we see in the philosophy of politics is an examination of the principles upon which legal and political systems are founded. Human rights, justice, fairness, social contract, democracy – these are all terms that can be examined by the philosopher in order to clarify exactly what they imply.

Once you get beyond Hobbes' view that society is constructed for mutual protection, once you say that it is **right** to organise society in a particular way, not just that it is necessary for survival to do so, then you imply ideas of justice, of freedom, of equality, of the valuation of human life, and of the place of human life within an understanding of the world as a whole.

A GENERAL POINT:

Philosphy grows and develops as an organic whole:

- How you organise society depends on your basic view of ethics.
- Ethics in turn depends on your view of the self and of what it means to be an individual human being.
- 'The self' has implications for the more general questions about the meaning and value of life that are explored in the philosophy of religion.
- Religious issues arise out of the fundamental questions about life – questions like 'What can I know for certain?,' 'Why is there anything rather than nothing?', 'What is life for?', 'What should I do?' that are the starting point for all philosophy.

7

THE SCOPE OF PHILOSOPHY TODAY

This book has of necessity been very selective. It has examined some of the major issues in philosophy, but has not really been able to show the breadth of philosophy as it is practised today. Nor has it been possible to include all the major philosophers of the past. Some, for example Hegel or Frege, have been very influential indeed, but there has been no room to include them, and they certainly deserve more than a brief mention if their thought is to be taken at all seriously. Most histories of philosophy offer an introduction to their work.

This final chapter simply attempts to fill a few of the gaps by offering a sketch of some other areas of philosophy, and some thinkers who are important for understanding the range of interests found in philosophy today.

First of all, the philosophy considered in this book is Western philosophy; it has not been possible to touch on Eastern philosophies. So, for example, the chapter on Mind and Body could have explored the Indian concept of the *atman*, or the Buddhist view that the self has no permanent reality, but is a conventional notion used to describe our constantly changing ideas, experiences and responses. Eastern philosophy is vast and fascinating, and it is important that those who are involved in Western philosophy should recognise that theirs is not the only way to approach these issues.

There are also whole branches of philosophy which it has not been possible to include (e.g. the Philosophy of Language or the Philosophy of Education), and there are also new approaches to philosophy (e.g. Feminist Philosophy). The fact that these have not found a place in this introduction does not imply any judgement about their value; rather, those covered so far form a bedrock of thought from which a student can move more easily into these other fields and are also the most immediately relevant to examination courses.

In order to give some further idea of the scope of philosophy, however, this chapter will look briefly two other branches of philosophy – Aesthetics and Formal Logic – and then at some aspects of what is known as modern 'Continental' philosophy.

Aesthetics

Most areas of philosophy spring from a simple but fundamental question: epistemology is the attempt to answer 'What can we know?'; political philosophy answers 'What is justice?' Aesthetics addresses the questions 'What is beauty?' and 'What is art?'

You can trace these questions through the whole history of philosophy, from Greek ideas of art, through medieval and Reformation debates about religious images (whether they pointed beyond themselves, or were in danger of being themselves worshipped in an idolatrous way), through Hume's attempt to get a norm of taste and Kant's analysis of the aesthetic experience, to Marxist critiques of art in terms of its social and political function, and on to existentialist and postmodernist views of art.

Aesthetics links with other areas of philosophy. For example, writing in the USA in the 1950s both the theologian Paul Tillich and philosopher Susanne Langer spoke of art as symbol – as pointing beyond itself to some other transcendent reality. This links aesthetics with the philosophy of religion. Indeed, Tillich held that all religious ideas and images were symbols, pointing to 'being-itself', and that religious truths could not be conveyed other than by symbols. A work of art could therefore be seen as in some sense 'religious', however secular its context, since it pointed to that which was beyond ordinary experience.

The work of the artist also links with the nature of the self, the nature of language and the nature of perception. A novelist, for example, may use language in a rich and subtle way in order to convey a whole range of emotions and intuitions; and not just to convey them, but to evoke them in the reader. A work of fiction thus invites an emotional and imaginative response. No two readers 'picture' the events described in the novel in exactly the same way. This is in contrast to a work of philosophy, which presents an argument with as much clarity as possible: it is clean, precise, straightforward; while the novel or poem is rich, evocative, symbolic and often deliberately ambiguous.

For reflection:

Plato was hostile to art and in favour of strict censorship. He saw art as subversive, replacing reality with fantasy, manipulating the emotions. Yet his dialogues are great works of literature; they are art!

- How can you allow art to have its full effect on the person who sees, reads or hears it, and yet maintain some rational control on what art says?

- Should art be politically correct? Marx saw art as having a social and political function. Good art, from a Marxist perspective, is that which reflects the values of social revolution, and which stirs the emotions in line with certain political values and attitudes.

- Is a work of art its own justification? If so, does it make any sense to speak of good art or bad?

The range of problems associated with aesthetics may be illustrated by the practical dilemma of whether or not you are able to call something a work of art:

Example:

I visit the home of a wealthy friend who tells me that he has just invested in a new work of art. I glance out of the window, and see a pile of bricks and rubble on his lawn. My friend has noticed me looking towards the lawn, and the glow of pride on his face leaves me in no doubt that the load of bricks and rubble is indeed his new work of art!

- He sees a work of art; I see a pile of rubble. It there any objective way of deciding between these two views ('seeing as')?

- If I agree that it is a work of art, where is that 'art' located? Is it in the art object (analysed as a pile of bricks and rubble)? Is it in the mind of the artist? Is its beauty, as the saying goes, in the eye of the beholder? Is art something that takes place in a triangular relationship: artist, art object, person appreciating it 'as' art?

- Is it pointing to something beyond itself – some feature of reality that I cannot describe literally, but which I sense by looking at the work of art? Or is it simply being itself, and inviting me to give it my attention? And is the act of giving attention itself an aesthetic experience?

- Would the pile of bricks remain art, even if nobody appreciated it as such?

- What emotions does it evoke in me? If only irritation and embarrassment, are these still valid as an aesthetic experience?

- The pile of bricks on the lawn is part of an artificial social construction – an artist making a living; an investor wanting a new 'piece'; a financial deal. Is art still art if it becomes an investment commodity?

- What is the nature of artistic imagination?

- Does the artist create an illusion, trying to make me see something more than that which is actually before my eyes?

- If the artist thought of it as one thing and I see it as something else, are there two works of art here, or only one?

Different periods have explored different aspects of art. In the eighteenth century, for example, primacy was given to natural beauty, and a sense of balance between nature and the mind perceiving nature. Kant saw a 'formal purposiveness' in those things that produced an aesthetic experience: art objects creating a sense of harmonious pleasure in the mind. The twentieth century has been more concerned with the nature of artistic production, and the process of artistic creativity has often become its own subject matter. Art reflects the particular self-understanding of each age, and this enables aesthetics to link with many other areas of philosophy.

Formal logic

Logic is the branch of philosophy which examines the process of reasoning. The basic structure of reasoning is that you start with a set of premises and reach a conclusion from them; the process of doing this is called **deductive logic.** An argument is **valid** if it is impossible for the conclusions to be false if the premises are true. An argument can be valid even if the premises are false (and therefore the conclusion is false); just because you are mistaken, it does not mean that your reasoning is not logical. An argument where the premises are true and the logic is valid is **sound**.

> ## NOTE:
>
> Deductive logic differs from the 'inductive' method of reasoning used by science. The inductive method starts with evidence and concludes that (on the balance of probability) this or that is to be expected in the future. A conclusion reached by that method is always open to be revised if there is new evidence. Deductive logic is not about evidence; it is the formal and abstract way of looking at the structure of an argument.

Logic can become very complex, with parts of an argument depending on others: 'if not this, then that, but if that then something else ...' Clearly, it would be cumbersome to write out all the elements of each argument in order to examine the logic involved.

To overcome this problem, formal logic uses an artificial form of language. This language uses sets of letters, A, B, C, etc., to stand for the various component premises and conclusions, and also a set of signs to act as connectives. These signs stand for such logical steps as 'and', 'or', 'it is not the case that', 'if...then' and 'if and only if'. This use of artificial languages is particularly associated with the philosopher Frege (1848-1925).

> **Example:**
>
> The connective 'if ... then' is shown by an arrow pointing to the right), the conclusion (therefore) is shown as a semi-colon.
>
> Take this argument:

I have missed the train. If I miss the train I arrive late at work. Therefore I shall arrive late at work.

We can formalise this by using the letter 'A' for 'I have missed the train' and 'B' for 'I will arrive late at work'.

Re-written, the argument becomes:

A, (A—>B);B

One important feature of logic is that it breaks down each sentence into its component parts and makes clear the relationship between them. So formal logic helps to clarify exactly what is and what is not valid. As you may imagine, the arguments set out in this way become very complex indeed, and there are a large number of unfamiliar signs used for the various connectives. If you pick up a copy of *The Journal of Symbolic Logic* and browse through it, you are likely to see page after page of what looks like advanced mathematics or complex scientific formulae. For the uninitiated, it is quite impossible to follow!

—— 'Continental' philosophy ——

For much of the twentieth century, there has been a division within Western philosophy, relating both to the way of doing philosophy and the sort of subjects covered. Most philosophers may be described as belonging either to the 'analytic' (or 'Anglo-American') or the 'Continental' tradition of philosophy.

- The analytic philosophers are mainly from the United States and Britain. They are concerned particularly with the meaning of statements and the way in which their truth can be verified, and with using philosophy as an analytic tool to examine and show the presuppositions of our language and thought. Well known philosophers in this school today would include Quine, Putnam, Searle, Rawls, Hampshire and Strawson. It also includes many philosophers already mentioned, including Russell, Ryle and Ayer. The twentieth century philosophy described so far in this book has come from this tradition.

- 'Continental' philosophy is a term which may be used to describe a range of philosophers from mainland Europe whose work is generally considered separately in courses on philosophy, although they do have relevance to the basic issues considered already. They include Husserl (1858-1938), whose **phenomenology** has influences many other continental philosophers, Heideggar and Sartre (**existentialism**) and, more recently, Lacan, Derrida and others. It is in this 'Continental' school that we meet the terms **structuralism**, **postmodernism** and **hermeneutics** (the study of interpretation: a term originally used of the study of scriptures, but now used more generally into the way in which any text is examined). Continental philosophy often reflects an intellectual approach to the creative arts in general, rather than something that is limited to the more narrowly defined tasks of the analytic school.

Whilst there is no space in this book to give an adequate account of the thinkers of the continental tradition, a brief outline of some of the main themes may serve to set it within the context of philosophy as a whole. This is important, because today there is far more mingling of the concerns of the two schools than was the case a few years ago.

Phenomenology

Husserl (1859-1938), like Descartes, wanted to find the basis of knowledge, making philosophy a 'rigorous science' that was founded on necessary truths independent of all presuppositions. His most important work was *Logical Investigations* (published in two volumes in 1900 and 1901). In this he declared that, for certainty, we had to start with our own conscious awareness. What is it that we actually experience? Husserl suggested that every mental act is directed towards an 'intentional object': what the mind is thinking about, whether or not that object exists.

Examples:

- I want to eat a cake. I need physical cake if I am going to eat; but thinking about a cake requires only an 'intentional object' – indeed, I am especially likely to think about a cake when there is no actual cake to be had!

- If I reflect on feeling depressed. Depression is an 'intentional object' of my thought, although there is no external object corresponding to it. Someone may say 'depression is nothing, it doesn't exist'; but for me, at that moment, it **is** real.

Husserl takes the subject matter of philosophy to be these 'objects of consciousness': whatever it is that we experience, quite apart from any questions about whether or not it exists in an objective, external world. Phenomenology also seeks to strip individual objects of all that makes them particular, seeking the pure essence – what they share with other objects of the same sort. (In many ways, this reflects Plato's idea of the 'forms'.) These fundamental 'essences', he argues, are known by intuition. As soon as we think about something, it takes on meaning for us because of the various essences by which we understand it. I have a consciousness of 'tree' as a pure essence, and as soon as I see (or think about) an actual tree, that essence is there to give it meaning for me.

Examples:

A child is shown a number of red objects. The mother says 'That's red.' The child automatically sorts out the common denominator of the experience, and quickly grasps the pure essence 'red'. When subsequently presented with objects of the same colour, the essence 'red' is already there, and becomes one of a number of essences by which any new object is understood. More sophisticated, the artist will play with unusual shades of red, testing out the 'horizon', the limits of the essence 'red'. Is it red, or is it really magenta? Add a touch more blue to the paint: now how do we see it?

Husserl argued that consciousness required three things:

1. a self (what he called the 'transcendental ego');
2. a mental act;
3. an object of that mental act.

Objects become objects of consciousness only when they have been given meaning and significance. An object is only understood (only really 'seen') once the mind has gone to work on it and given it meaning in terms of its pure essences. Everything is therefore dependent on the 'transcendental ego' for its meaning and significance. Once we encounter the world, we start to give it meaning, we start to interpret it in terms of pure essences; in other words, we start to deal with it in terms of its 'objects of consciousness'.

One reason why Husserl has been so important for continental philosophy is that he allowed questions of meaning and value, and the whole range of emotions and other experiences, to become the valid subject matter of philosophy. In other words, continental philosophers were set free to explore many aspects of life that appeared closed to those of the analytic tradition, who remained primarily concerned with language.

Existentialism

Existentialism is the name given to the branch of philosophy which is concerned with the meaning of human existence - its aims, its significance and overall purpose – and the freedom and creative response to life made by individuals.

Notice how this follows on from phenomenology. If philosophy is free to deal with consciousness and the actions which spring from it, it can explore human self-awareness and self-doubt, and the actions and events that give meaning to life. Two important philosophers for the development of existentialism are Heidegger (1889-1976), see especially *Being and Time* (1927), and Sartre (1905-1980), see *Being and Nothingness* (1943).

A central feature of existentialism is that it is concerned with the way in which human beings relate to the world. Much philosophy examines external objects and the minds that comprehend them as though the two were separable; the mind just observing the world in a detached way. Existentialism, by contrast, starts from the basis of the self as involved, as engaged with the world. We seek to understand things because we have to deal with them and find the meaning and significance of our own life among them.

An example:

You pick up a hammer and start hammering a nail. You do not first think about the hammer and then decide how to use it; you use it automatically. Your mind is engaged with the activity of hammering. Heidegger sees this as a **ready-to-hand** way of dealing with things: not as an observer, but as an engaged individual.

Husserl had attempted, by bracketing out any particular features and trying to see only the pure essences of a phenomenon, to get a generally acceptable view of things. Existentialism moved away from that position by emphasising that there is always an element of personal engagement – a particular point of view. This raises the general philosophical question about whether every view is a view from a particular perspective, carrying with it the values and understanding of the person who has it. The alternative is a 'view from nowhere': a view that does not take a personal viewpoint into account. But is that possible?

For Heidegger, we are 'thrown' into the world, and our main experience of *Dasein* ('being there') is 'concern', in the sense that some of the objects we encounter in the world are more important for us than others, and so we become involved with them. Heidegger argued that we are what we take ourselves to be; we do not have a fixed human nature. You live in an **authentic** way if you take each situation as it comes and show your true nature through what you do. Otherwise you try to escape from the anxiety of being true to yourself by conforming to what others expect of you.

For Sartre, particular things (as opposed to an understanding of it in general categories) take on importance. In his novel *Nausea,* individual things appear just as they are, and refuse to be categorised. There is also the sense that a person is radically free; in just the same way that individual things are not totally known by their essences, so a person is not totally controlled by duties and responsibilities. Such freedom can be a threat, it produces a disorientation, a nausea.

FOR REFLECTION:

Look back at the chapter on Mind and Body. We are defined by many things, and by the various roles that we take on. But can we ever be fully defined in this way? Is there a self that refuses to be categorised; that insists on the freedom to be unique?

Sartre has three kinds of being.

1. **Being-in-itself.** This is the being of non-human objects, things just exist as they are.
2. **Being-for-itself.** At the level of consciousness or self-awareness, a being is aware of the world around it, of other things that are not

itself. If we are self aware, we cannot be reduced to a thing-in-itself, e.g. I may work as a postman, but I am not fully described as 'postman' (as a thing-in-itself) because, as a human being, I am always more than any such description. If people treat me simply as 'postman' they dehumanise me, they take from me the distinctive thing that makes me a person.

3. **Being-for-others.** As human beings, we form relationships and express our human nature through them. Relating to others, and aware of our own freedom, we are able to live in an 'authentic' way: we are being fully ourselves.

IN OTHER WORDS:

- Phenomenology allows human experiences and responses to become a valid object of philosophical study.
- Existentialism explores the way in which people relate to the world, including issues of value, meaning and purpose; it is about engagement, not detached observation.
- If I act out a role, I am not engaged with the whole of myself. To be authentic, I act in a way which reflects my self-awareness, and the awareness of my own freedom. This is who I am; this is what I choose to do; this is the real me.

Structuralism

The main theme of structuralism is that you can only understand something once you relate it to the wider structures within which it operates. Things are defined primarily in terms of their relationships with others. Structuralist approaches were developed in the philosophy of language and in anthropology, associated particularly with Saussure and Levi-Strauss, but spread into many different cultural areas.

Examples:

- To understand a word, consider its meaning in terms of other words and the language as a whole.
- To understand a political statement, look at the politician, how he or she is to stay in power, what the media expects, what effect he or she needs to make with this statement.
- A 'soundbite' or a newspaper headline can only really be

understood in terms of the structure of the paper or the broadcast within which it is set.

In Husserl's phenomenology there was an independent self that existed prior to the encounter with the phenomena: the 'transcendental ego'. Existentialism focused on that self, especially in its freedom and choices in its engagement with the world. Structuralism (and particularly its later development, known as 'post-structuralism') is a reaction against the importance given to this 'self' – structures and relationships now take priority.

Jacques Lacan (1900-80) argued that we do not first become fully formed individuals and then start to express our individuality through language, but we become individuals (we develop our personalities, if you like) through the use of language. And that language, with its ideas and its grammar, pre-dates us. We don't make it up as we go along; we inherit it.

Lacan was primarily a psychoanalyst, and it is interesting to reflect that in psychoanalysis it is through a free flow of ideas that thoughts and feelings buried in the unconscious may appear. The flow of language is not controlled by the ego. Indeed, it is in order to heal and change the ego that the analysis is taking place. The subject emerges through language. For Lacan, it would seem that if there is no speech, then there is no subject, but he goes further; there are no metaphysical entities at all. God, for example, is a function of the 'Other' in language, not something that exists outside language.

Two features of a structuralist/post-structuralist approach:

1. There is no transcendent self that has some pure idea which it wants to convey, and which is later, imperfectly translated into a medium of communication – spoken, written or visual. Rather the meaning is just exactly what is spoken or written. It is to be understood in terms of the structures of communication, not with reference to some outside author. A story does not **have** a meaning; a story **is** its meaning.

2. To understand a piece of writing, one should carry out a process of **deconstruction**, laying bare the presuppositions of the text, and comparing what an author claims to be saying with the actual form of language used and the sometimes contradictory claims that such a written form implies. Deconstruction has been developed

particularly by Jacques Derrida (b.1930), an influential figure in this movement. Deconstruction is the attempt to deal with the end of metaphysics. For Derrida, there is no external or fixed meaning to a text, nor it there a subject who exists prior to language and prior to particular experiences. **You cannot get outside or beyond the structure.**

Derrida is concerned with 'actuality' – with being in touch with present events. The following extracts are from an interview in which he starts with an explanation of his term 'artifactuality'.

[Artifactuality] means that actuality is indeed *made*: it is important to know what it is made of, but it is even more necessary to recognise that it is made. It is not given, but actively produced; it is sorted, invested and performatively interpreted by a range of hierarchising and selective procedures – factitious or artifactual procedures which are always subservient to various powers and interests of which their 'subjects' and agents (producers and consumers of actuality, always interpreters and in some cases 'philosophers' too), are never sufficiently aware.

In other words, the information we receive is not neutral, but is the product of the structures by which the media operate. This has practical consequences:

Hegel was right to tell the philosophers of his time to read the newspapers. Today the same duty requires us to find out how news is made, and by whom: the daily papers, the weeklies, and the TV news as well. We need to insist on looking at them from the other end: that of the press agencies as well as that of the tele-prompter. And we should never forget what this entails: whenever a journalist or a politician appears to be speaking to us directly, in our homes, and looking us straight in the eye, he or she is actually reading, from a screen, at the dictation of a 'prompter', and reading a text which was produced elsewhere, on a different occasion, possibly by other people, or by a whole network of nameless writers and editors.'

(From 'The Deconstruction of Actuality' an interview with Derrida, published in *Radical Philosophy*, Autumn 1994, p.28.)

But Derrida warns against 'neo-idealism': the idea that nothing really happens, that all is an illusion just because it is set within a structure by the media. Rather, he wants to emphasise that deconstruction is about getting down to an event, to a 'singularity', to what is irreducible and particular in an individual happening.

IN OTHER WORDS:

- To understand anything, look at its relationships and the structure within which it is set.
- There is no subject that exists prior to language. I may think of something before I write it, but even that act of thinking borrows from a whole tradition of language and thought.
- News comes to us through the media; it is the product of a process by which information is sorted and expressed in particular ways, often for a particular purpose. Real events are unique, reports of them put them into categories and start to colour our interpretation of them.

Postmodernism

Postmodernism is a rather vague term for a number of approaches to philosophy, literature and the arts, which have in common a rejection of an earlier 'modernist' view. The 'modern' view, against which postmodernism reacts, is one that sees the image as the production of the unique human subject. Existentialism in particular is focused on the self, its freedom, and the choices by which it creates itself and its world. Structuralism has disputed this 'modern' belief in the primacy of the humanist imagination as a creative source of meaning.

Postmodernism is a term used beyond the writings of Derrida, Lyotard and others who work in the fields of philosophy and literary criticism, for it can apply to all the arts. Indeed, the ideas were explored in architecture before transferring to philosophy. Previously, an image could be taken to refer to something external, in the 'real' world or in human consciousness. In postmodernism, an image reflects only other images – it has no fixed reference. There is therefore no 'authentic' image; authentic in the sense that an existentialist would use that term.

A message is, for postmodernism, no longer sent from a creative author to a receptive reader. Rather, it is bound up with a mass of reduplication. We shuffle and arrange images, but do not have any creative control over them. In a work of art, a novel or a film, a postmodernist approach undermines the modernist belief in the image as the product of an individual consciousness.

A postmodern image displays its own artificial nature. It clearly represents – but without depth. So, for example, in the art world, one might contrast Picasso (who, as a 'modernist' strove for a unique view and form of communication) with Warhol's use of mass-produced public images. (An interesting discussion of this is found in R Kearney – 'The Crisis of the Postmodernist Image' – in *Contemporary French Philosophy* ed. A Phillips Griffiths Cambridge, 1987.)

FOR REFLECTION:

Modernism: The dilemma and existential agony of the blank sheet of paper, a set of paints and brushes, and the desire to express oneself through a unique image.

Postmodernism: The word-processing package comes to the rescue, for it contains a variety of pieces of 'clip art' which can be instantly printed out, copied and arranged on the paper.

Postmodernism is encouraged by the developments in technology – particularly mass communication and the ability to reproduce images. The individual subject is no longer considered to be the creator of his or her images. What we appear to create is what is already there around us. We produce consumer items. It is not so much philosophy that is postmodern, but the whole of society. There are many images to be shuffled, but there is no metaphysical insight to be had, and no transcendental reality to represent.

This is also reflected in the postmodernist view, explored by Jean-Francois Lyotard, that statements about the overall purpose of life or society (e.g. 'society exists for the benefit of its members'), sometimes called 'metanarratives', are losing their credibility. It is no longer realistic to make a general statements of a metaphysical nature about life, since they do not reflect the fragmented nature of modern society.

IN OTHER WORDS:

For postmodernism, you cannot get behind the images, symbols and reproduced goods of a technological age in order to discern individuality, purpose or meaning. In other words, it is a view devoid of what was traditionally known as 'metaphysics'.

A final example:

I am the author of this book: I address you, the reader, directly in order to illustrate some the issues connected with structuralism and the postmodern outlook.

What do you think of me as an author? You could say 'He's just stuck together bits of information that others have given him.' That is true. You could go on to say 'There is absolutely nothing original in it!' This is a more serious charge, but made complicated because there is a certain originality in the way that the ideas of others are selected, analysed, arranged and presented.

But suppose I claim to have said something original. Can that claim be justified?

- What of the words I use? Their meanings are given by the society that uses this language (if they weren't, you would not understand them). They do not originate in my mind.
- What of the climate of opinion within which I write? Does that not shape my views? Am I responsible for it, or shaped by it?
- And what of comments for which I claim originality? If you knew everything that I had read, everyone that I had spoken to, could you not predict my views? Could you not analyse my views, show influences, categorise the style, place my views within a particular tradition. A literary critic often shows that what seems to be a unique expression of a thinking self is in fact an intellectual patchwork of influences.
- This book is being written to fit 192 printed pages of a particular size, and in a particular style. Its chapters reflect some examination syllabuses; suggestions about content have been made by professional readers; various things have been asked for by editors. What is said is determined by the constraints of space, purpose and market.
- Thus the author of this book can vanish!

Personal note: I may keep within the overall structure of language, but I feel that, from time to time, I am entitled to peer round the side of the structure and address you, the reader, directly. It is this that structuralism denies. Indeed, the idea of an author making a personal appeal to a reader is just another literary device. I disappear again!

—— Where is philosophy going? ——

Philosophy does not remain static, it is therefore reasonable to at least ask if philosophy is moving in any particular direction at the moment. A recent article by Nicholas Rescher of the University of Pittsburgh in *The Review of Metaphysics* examined such trends in philosophy in the United States. He found that the subject was in a healthy state, with over 10,000 practising philosophers in the USA and Canada. While he could detect no single direction to philosophy, he found that the older divisions between 'Anglo-American' (analytic) and 'Continental' philosophy were perceived as being on the wane.

Of particular aspects of philosophy, he noted (and a browse through recent journals can confirm) that the History of Philosophy continues to be popular, with studies of Leibniz, Hume, Kant, Nietzsche and others. Many of these philosophers have societies devoted to their study.

Of the general themes in philosophy pursued today, he noted particularly:

- 'persons';
- ethics;
- Artificial Intelligence;
- feminist issues;
- social and economic issues;
- maths and formal logic.

He also noted a major growth in applied philosophy: that is, philosophy applied to specialist areas, such as law, computer use and science. Rescher's list does not exhaust the areas of philosophical interest, but at least it may serve to give a clue to the range of current issues and topics on which philosophers are working.

POSTSCRIPT

Philosophy is an activity, not just a body of knowledge or a list of problems to be solved. A philosopher is one who takes a contemporary problem (and all problems that are not yet resolved are contemporary, even if they were originally considered by Plato!), looks at the meaning of the terms used, the structure and nature of the language in which the problem is couched, the logic involved with various attempted answers, and the overall place that the problem has within an understanding of life.

Of course, different philosophers will take different approaches. Linguistic philosophy will concentrate on the meaning, structure and validation of the language used. Existential philosophy will examine the place of that question within an overall understanding of life and its meaning. Metaphysics will look at the overall structures of existence and the way the question is related to them. Structuralism will expose the context of the problem and the linguistic, political, social and structures through which the problem is encountered.

Because it is an activity, philosophy thrives on puzzles and dilemmas. They are the food that sustains its life. The aim of this book has been to open up some of those puzzles, and to give just a hint at the way in which philosophers of the past have tackled them. By its very nature, philosophy remains a discipline in which all its findings are open to revision. The only final conclusion that can be reached, therefore, is the value of the task.

Let us return to one of the greatest images in the history of Western philosophy – Plato's analogy of the cave. Breaking free from the chains that limit his vision and turning to look up towards the mouth of the cave, the philosopher starts to perceive things as they really are, rather than the shadows they cast on the on the wall of the cave. But the progress upwards is painful, and the philosopher is literally dragged out of the cave and into the sunlight. It takes time to adjust the eyes, to see clearly, to look at the sun. Seeing reality itself, rather than the puppet show of life which the prisoners in the cave take to represent reality, is initially painful and confusing.

Enlightenment is a gradual and difficult process; it can seem irrelevant to those still besotted by the picture show deep in the cave; it can lead to confusion and self-doubt. Plato's conviction is that once reality itself is perceived, nothing can ever be quite the same again, and that perception, however fleeting, remains the source of wisdom.

Philosophers need the humility to acknowledge the tentative and provisional nature of their claims. So let the final words, and my own conclusion to this book, be those of Plato. Before giving his interpretation of the analogy of the cave, he says:

> Heaven knows whether it is true; but this, at any rate, is how it appears to me.

FURTHER READING

The books listed here are a limited, personal selection of those which should prove useful as a follow-up to issues touched on in this book. They are in addition to the books already referred to in the text, and to the original philosophical texts.

For a historical overview of Western Philosophy:

Hamlyn, D W *A History of Western Philosophy*, Viking, 1987; Penguin, 1990 A good basic history of philosophy.

Shand, John *Philosophy and Philosophers*, Penguin Books, 1994 A good overview from an historical perspective, touching on the major issues in philosophy.

History of Philosophy HarperCollins College Outline, USA, 1993 Clear, concise entries on the major contributions of each philosopher, arranged historically; very useful for quick reference or revision, less so for those wanting an historical introduction to a particular theme.

Kenny, Anthony ed. *The Illustrated History of Philosophy*, Oxford, 1994 A useful and authoritative historical survey for the reader who does not attempt to rely heavily on the illustrations!

Of the older histories, my personal preference would be **Bertrand Russell's** *History of Western Philosophy*, Allen & Unwin, 1946, second edition 1961. It is incisive, witty and readable; giving a vast panorama of philosophy, with particular reference to the social and political circumstances of philosophers, from the pre-Socratics to the early years of the twentieth century.

Other useful books for giving an idea of the whole scope of philosophy:

O'Hear, A *What Philosophy Is*, Penguin, 1985 Valuable as a general introduction, with good sections on epistemology, metaphysics and language.

Flew, A *An Introduction to Western Philosophy*, Thames and Hudson, revised edition 1989 A very substantial introduction!

Murdoch, Iris *Metaphysics as a Guide to Morals* Chatto & Windus, 1992 This book is much wider in its scope than the title might at first glance suggest. There are particularly valuable sections here on consciousness and thought (relevant for our section on Mind) and on the traditional arguments for the existence of God. There is also a chapter on Will and Duty. A solid but stimulating book on a whole range of philosophical and religious issues, but those new to philosophy may find it quite difficult going in places.

Magee, Bryan *Men of Ideas*, BBC Books, 1978
Magee, Bryan *The Great Philosophers*, BBC Books, 1987
These books are transcripts of television interviews with modern philosphers. Magee's introductions and summaries are a model of clarity, and the earlier of the books gives a good overview of twentieth century philosophy up to the mid 1970s.

For quick reference, and for checking on the meaning of philsophical terms and which thinkers are associated with them, there are many valuable dictionaries of philosophy.

Journals offer a broad view of the way in which philosophy is practised today. They vary greatly in terms of their accessibility to the general reader. The most readable of these for the newcomer to philosophy would seem to be *Philosophy Now*, published quarterly. There is also *Radical Philosophy*, a journal of Socialist and Feminist Philosophy, published bi-monthly.

University libraries are likely to have a whole range of quarterly journals from both Britain, America and the Continent.

The British ones to examine are: *Mind* (published by Oxford University Press), *Philosophy* (published by Cambridge University Press) and *Philosophical Quarterly* (published by Blackwell publishers). Among American journals are: *Philosophy Today* and *The Review of Metaphysics*. As in all academic subjects, the quarterly journals tend to be the vehicles by which professional philosophers communicate with one another. They seldom have scope to offer enough background information for those who are not already familiar with the issues being considered. Some journals are almost unreadable to those not already well versed in their particular branch of philosophy. *The Journal of Symbolic Logic*, for example, is not intended for the casual reader!

GLOSSARY

The following are a selection of terms used in this book, gathered here for quick reference. For more information on each of them, please refer to the relevant Index entry.

Behaviourism the view that the mind can be understood in terms of physical activity

Blik a particular way of seeing something, used especially of religious language

Categorical imperative sense of moral obligation; the basis of Kant's moral argument for the existence of God

Cosmological (arguments) arguments for the existence of God, based on observation of the world

Deconstruction the process of examining a text in the context of the linguistic and social structures within which it was put together (see structuralism)

Deductive argument an argument based on logical principles, rather than on the assessment of evidence

Dualism the view that mind and matter are distinct and separate (of importance for the mind/body problem, but also for epistemology)

Empiricism a theory of knowledge based on sense experience

Epiphenomenalism the theory that the mind is a product of complex physical processes

Epistemology the theory of knowledge

Idealism fundamentally, reality is mental

Inductive method the process of coming to a conclusion based on evidence

Interactionism the general term for theories of the mind in which mind and body are distinct (dualism) but interact.

Intuitive knowledge direct knowledge which is not the result of conscious reasoning or experience

Materialism reality is material (e.g. the 'self' is a way of describing the body and its actions)

Metaphysics the study of the structures of reality

Modernism a general term for the self-conscious approach to philosophy and the arts, developed particularly in the first half of the twentieth century

Natural selection Darwin's theory of evolution, but which only the strongest examples of a species survive to breed

Numinous the 'holy' beyond rational definition (term used by Rudolph Otto)

Ontological (argument) argument for the existence of God, based simply on a proposed definition of God and independent of evidence

Panentheism belief that God exists within everything (implied by theism, but not the same as pantheism)

Pantheism the idea that God is identical with the material universe

Phenomenology the study of what is experienced (a theory developed by Husserl)

Postmodernism a modern, 'Continental' approach to philsophy and the arts, rejecting the modernist concept of a self-conscious, authentic, creative self in favour of a direct appreciation of symbols and texts in their cultural context. See also structuralism.

Pragmatism the idea that a theory should be assessed according to its pracical use

Rationalism theory of knowledge based on the action of the mind

Reductionism the tendency to reduce everything to its component parts; the 'nothing but' view of complex things

Schema a cluster of rational terms by which the 'holy' is understood and described (the process is called 'schematisation')

Structuralism an approach to philosophy, developed within the 'Continental' school in the second half of the twentieth century, which interprets the meaning of a text, a word or an idea in the context of the structures of thought within which it is found

Theism belief in the existence of God

Utilitarianism the ethical theory that evaluates actions in terms of their prediced results ('the greatest good to the greatest number')

Verification checking the validity of a statement, used especially of logical positivist and other empirical approaches to language.

INDEX